# The Internet Joke Book

edited by Brad Templeton

Published by

Peer-to-Peer Communications, Inc.

Published by Peer-to-Peer Communications, Inc.
    P.O. Box 640218
    San Jose
    California 95164-0218, U.S.A.
    Phone: 800-420-2677
    Fax: 408-435-0895

Cover: John Klossner, Klossner Studios, CT
Printing: George Lithograph, Brisbane, CA

Printed in the United States of America
2   3   4   5   6   7   8   9   10


ISBN 1-57398-025-0

# TABLE OF CONTENTS

# In the Beginning

**What's a "rec.humor.funny?"**

Unless you're under a rock, you've been reading a lot today about *the Internet* — the world-wide network of networks that some people tout as the foundation of the information superhighway of the future. The Internet has caught the public attention because it's not just a communications medium, it's also a place. People meet and interact there, communicating with one another and holding discussions on thousands of topics.

While you may have just heard about it or perhaps even joined it, the Internet has been going in one way or another for 25 years, and a complex culture has developed. What you may not know is that comedy plays a large part in that culture.

Have you ever wondered how jokes spread around the world? How a simple joke can zoom around the entire country in just a few days? You're about to discover a part of the answer. That answer is that, to a small extent, it happens on the Internet, and *I do it.*

I publish an on-line electronic humour magazine over a computer network called USENET — the electronic conferencing network of the Internet. Each day, scores of people from all over the world send us the latest (and not so latest) jokes that they have heard. We pick the best ones and send them out over the network. They estimate that over 500,000 people, spread all over the world, read the jokes that we select. (I say "we" because while I did the editing and selection from 1987 to mid-1992, the job was passed on to Maddi Hausmann Sojourner in 1992 and she's done the editing since then.)

You have in your hands a special jokebook with the very best material from the first five years of that electronic humour publication. Each year, a special book was produced with the best material from that year and sold to the network audience. Now, we've taken the top 25% of the first four books to make one very special book of the best in Internet humour.

This book contains the jokes, with notes at the top to indicate who submitted them, where they are from and how the jokes were rated. About 40% of the book is devoted to jokes about computers, science, math, academia and "the net" itself, while the other chapters contain the best in comedy on general subjects as selected for the network audience.

The jokes are written in the submitter's own words: any stylistic highs and lows were considered to add to the individuality of the joke and were not edited.

## Networks & USENET

Millions of people use computers today, and for many, one of the most important uses to which they put their computer is communicating with other *people*. The world is full of vast networks of computers, and while those networks are often used to send computer data around, one of the most common things they transmit is plain old text for people to read.

These days the network that has everybody's attention is the Internet, a vast collection of connected networks that spans the globe. Nobody owns or runs the Internet, but everybody's on it, including these days all the major online services. There are lots of applications that people use to communicate on the Internet, and when it comes to online discussions or "bulletin boards" their tool of choice is a system called USENET.

USENET is a totally unstructured network of close to 260,000 computers of all sizes. It exists solely for the communication of people. It has no single owner, and nobody runs it, but somehow it works.

There are over 10,000 discussion categories on USENET, and most of them allow anybody to write directly into the discussion. If you want to say something, you compose it on your keyboard and tell your computer to post it under a specific discussion category. (Discussion categories are called "newsgroups.") Your computer sends it to the computers that it talks to, and they tell two friends, and they tell two friends, and so on, and so on until the whole world has the message.

When you sit down to read, your computer will have collected all the messages that have come to it from other computers, and it presents them to you. The results are truly amazing, sometimes hyperactive discussions where none of the participants are present in the same place, or even at the same time.

## The Oral Tradition

In today's document-heavy world, jokes are the modern oral tradition. The USENET computer network is a unique merger of the oral and written modes. The medium is a written one, but the character of the discussion is very oral.

Since USENET's early days, it has had an unmoderated joke exchange called **rec.humor**, which might be categorized as, well... *too* oral. People just post anything they feel like there, without regard for whether it was posted last week by somebody else, and without regard for whether it should be in the newsgroup at all. Indeed, about 70% of the postings in **rec.humor** aren't jokes at all, but rather simply inanities or comments on jokes. (They also post without concern for spelling, grammar or punctuation.)

This led to my creation of an edited or "moderated" newsgroup. In such a group, all people who want to post send their messages to the moderator by electronic mail, and he or she posts them according to whatever rules have been set out.

Most USENET moderators take the rather thankless job of simply weeding out duplicates, misdirected messages and pointless diatribes, passing through all other messages without comment. I decided to do more. I wanted to edit for quality — to be more like a comedy newsmagazine than a bulletin board.

And thus, **rec.humor.funny** was born. The name was itself a joke on the **rec.humor** newsgroup's poor reputation. The motto was, *"It's like rec.humor, except it's funny."* Others had tried before with moderated joke mailing lists, but had failed. I'm proud to say that **rec.humor.funny** has been a success, and it rose to be the most widely read group not just on USENET but on any net. This book is your chance to see the results.

## Banned at Stanford?

In late 1988, a controversy exploded around **rec.humor.funny**. That controversy resulted in a long-term ban of most of the newsgroup at the University of Waterloo (your editor's alma mater) and a temporary ban at Stanford University. Coverage of the trouble was front page news.

*Why?*

A joke was published late in 1988 that wasn't encrypted in the usual way offensive jokes are encrypted. In spite of other warnings on the joke, a civil engineering grad student at MIT named Jonathan E. D. Richmond read, and was offended by, the joke. (To see the joke, look on page 176.)

He got *real* bothered by the joke, and went on a tirade on USENET to force me to change my editorial policy and ban offensive jokes. (My policy is not to judge jokes on their content and political correctness—only on how well written they are as comedy.) He threatened a mail barrage (I got 3 messages) and to call my employers (I'm self-employed.) When all else failed, he decided to go to the papers. There he got what he wanted.

**Rec.humor.funny** was fed out to the world via the University of Waterloo, which being the largest computer centre in the town I lived in, was my main link to USENET. Richmond found a reporter with the *K-W Record* (the local daily) who has a fondness for this sort of story. She made it front page news, with the headline "UW Computer system used to send racial jokes."

The stories continued for over a week, on the front page, and the front page of section 2. The paper pressured the University to shut off the newsgroup. Like most, I believed that it was antithetical to the nature of a university to tell people what they can and can't read, so it surprised me a bit when they complied. The UW President (Doug Wright) asked me to transmit no offensive jokes to them. I complied—they are, after all, the University's computers, and the President does have the right to say what goes through them.

In the meantime, Richmond also went to the Boston Herald, a tabloid. They printed the story (page 2) but not quite his way, to say the least. He learned a lesson about the press at that point and stopped his campaign.

Are the jokes so evil? You have them, so judge for yourself. There are some nasty jokes in this book. In the online world, however, they were all presented in a special code, forcing readers to run a decryption program on the jokes before they could be read.

## Not #1 on Earth

Thanks in part to the bannings and controversy and the growth of USENET and the Internet, **rec.humor.funny** became for some time the world's most widely read computerized forum! It is read daily on every continent—and that includes daily posting at the South Pole. However in mid 1991, a forum devoted to the discussion of (what else?) sex surged up the charts and became the leader. Another area devoted to job ads (on a network that some people mistakenly believe is non-commercial) is surging and has similar readership to **rec.humor.funny**.

Frivolous, you say? Perhaps—but underneath there is something deeper. Computer networks aren't just for sending bank transactions and software patches. They have the potential to link distant human beings, and to entertain. There's nothing more human than a good laugh. In the end, to what better purpose could we put our networks?

## Copyright

This collection is copyright © 1995 by Brad Templeton. All rights reserved.

How can I claim this on jokes I didn't write? I'm not. I'm claiming an "editor's" or "collection" copyright: copyright in the work done to select, edit, collect, correct, typeset and publish this work. This is the same sort of copyright that publishers of dictionaries claim — they don't own the individual words, but they do own the collection.

I am claiming no copyright on most of the individual jokes found here. Most of them are, to the best of my knowledge, copyrighted by their authors and used with permission or in the public domain. (It is possible that some of the jokes in here that have no attribution are actually copyrighted. This is the responsibility of each individual submitter. All submitters were asked to attribute their jokes, if at all possible. If any unfair misuse of copyright is present in this book, it was not wilful.)

Some are very short and attributed to comedians or other writers. In this case, all are excerpts from larger works, and reproduced under the news reporting and "fair use" clauses of copyright law. The original authors retain all rights in these jokes.

Some jokes are marked with the keyword original, or are otherwise copyrighted. Rights in these reside with the attributed author, and explicit or implicit permission for distribution to computer network readers has been given.

The editor's notes, introductions and other non-joke materials in this book are © 1995 Brad Templeton.

All this is well and good, but what does a collection copyright mean? It means that you can use the public domain jokes in this book, in small quantities, for your own purposes.

What you *can't* do is photocopy the book, or pages from it, or use it as a sourcebook for another collection. You can't take all, or even a substantial part of the jokes in this book, and use them as your own, even if you type them in yourself, unless you have explicit permission from me.

## The Joke Headers

If you look at the jokes, you will see they have all sorts of strange words and phrases under the title. This section tells you how to interpret these headers.

Each joke has a centered header that gives the title of the joke, the electronic "mailing address" and name of the person who sent it, and some information on the content and quality of the joke. Here's what you might see:

### THERE AND BACK AGAIN

bilbo@bagend.shire.org (Bilbo Baggins)
Hobbiton Computer Centre                                                          chuckle, heard it

The titles are straightforward. Sometimes they were chosen by the people who submitted the joke, but often they have been chosen by the editor.

### The Submitter's Address

If you're not a USENET user, the next line in every joke will be the hardest to understand. The names provided here are actually an *address* you would type to an electronic mail program if you wanted to send a message to one of these people on the Internet. These days almost everybody has a standard "at-sign" address, but in the early days there were other networks, which all used different addressing rules, characters and styles.

In general, E-mail addresses consist of three parts. A *user name* (The part to the left of a % or @, or to the right of an !) is the identification of a person on his or her own computer. This will usually be something like their first name, initials, last name or a nickname. You might consider a user name to be like a combination of a person's name and street address number.

A *site name* is the name of a computer on the electronic mail network. Roughly, this corresponds to a street name in the postal mail addresses that everybody is familiar with.

Finally a *domain* is usually a collection of computers. This is analogous to a city, state or country. (To get technical, a site is also called a domain.)

Full details on how to decode these names are beyond the scope of this book. Many of them are intuitively obvious — for example *harvard.edu* is Harvard University (in the educational hierarchy). Others, unfortunately, will look like gibberish to the uninitiated.

**Due to bugs in mail handling software all over the network, the editor cannot be held responsible for errors in mailing addresses shown.**

### The Organization

Sometimes under the name and mailing address you'll see the name of an organization or company to which the submitter belongs. Sometimes this is real, and sometimes a silly line has been filled in by the submitter.

The most important thing to remember is that these organization and company names are there only to help you identify the submitter and tell where he or she is from. NO SUBMITTER IS ACTING IN ANY WAY AS A SPOKESPERSON FOR THEIR ORGANIZATION OR COMPANY IN THIS JOKE-BOOK. Quite the opposite, in most cases, I'm very sure. These jokes are all submitted on people's private time, and aren't coming from AT&T (for example) or any other company on the net.

### Keywords

Below all this, in parentheses, you will see the joke keywords. These have been added by the editor.

These include quality keywords in the following order: maybe, smirk, chuckle, funny, laugh, sidesplit. I've been very conservative with giving away the latter two ratings.

You will also find "content" keywords that warn you about potential offensive material in the joke. You will find words like "sexual," "scatological," "swearing," or references to ethnic and sexual stereotypes in many jokes. (These are in no way complete descriptions on the possible offensive content of the jokes.)

You will also find keywords like "true" which mark that the submission is supposed to be a factual account, and "original," which means the the submitter (or someone close) actually wrote the joke.

The keyword "heard it" indicates that I felt the joke is moderately well known. The keyword "rot13" indicates a truly nasty joke. ("rot13" is the name of the cypher used to encode nasty jokes so that they can't be read without deliberate action.)

The keyword "topical" indicates that the joke refers to items in the news at the time it was submitted. These jokes are collected in their own chapter as well. Other keywords should explain themselves, and if they don't, don't worry.

Let me say once again that there are mistakes in the keywords, and it is entirely possible you will find sexual or offensive material in a joke that is not marked. These markings exist for your convenience only, and in no way guarantee the content or quality of a joke.

### Joke Bodies

You'll see various submitter's comments included with the jokes. Some of them may refer to antecedents you won't find in the book. Don't worry if you're confused. That's what reading the net is normally like.

You may also, from time to time, see various netter's words and symbols that are not used in the real world. One to watch out for is the "smiley-face." This looks like ":-)" and is to be viewed sideways. (Try it.) It indicates sarcasm, or says, "I'm kidding."

## Caveat Reador

Here's a message you'll see repeated many times throughout this book: **This is not a jokebook for children.** It contains many jokes with offensive words, explicit sexual references and racial or sexist, sick or offensive themes, and these jokes are so marked. If you are potentially offended by such material, do not read these jokes. If you do, you bring any offense upon yourself.

All jokes draw their humour from something in life that we fear. A jokebook that didn't poke fun at things dear to some people would not be much of a jokebook. If I excluded everything I got a complaint on, half these jokes would be missing.

In the case of the racial and sexist jokes, I have often included them because I laughed at their sheer offensiveness and audacity, which is to say I was laughing *at* the racism, not *with* it. Others are funny because a popular (if usually incorrect) stereotype is necessary in the construction of the joke. (Where this is not necessary, the term "<ethnic>" or "JEDR" is often used.) No personal slight is intended against any of the people or groups lampooned in this book. My editorial policies, explained on the net, actually seriously reduce the level of hateful humour on USENET.

In the end, I feel it is very important to be able to laugh at the evil in the world. I feel it is much better to have a world where we can do this freely than to have a world where nobody gets offended.

It's also worth noting that, because on USENET, people interact only through their written words, it is the world's first "community without colour." You can't tell a person's skin colour, weight or appearance unless they tell you about it. To longtime netters, race has left the arena of human interaction — and the stereotypes of the "old" world can be made fun of without harm, as long as no malice is involved.

## Thanks

Thanks first of all to all the wonderful submitters who made up or submitted these jokes. For those of you who didn't make it, keep trying. Thanks to *most* of you for handling rejection with grace.

Thanks to Grant Robinson and especially Harriett Hardman for helping proofread the various books. Thanks to George Doscher, Jane Ring and Barbara, my assistants while **rec.humor.funny** existed as the "TeleJoke" Round Table on the GEnie online service.

And thanks of course to Maddi Hausmann Sojourner, the current editor of **rec.humor.funny**, who also helped select the jokes in the last part of the Topical comedy chapter.

The joke archives (along with some great Science Fiction) are available on CD-ROM. Contact ClariNet Communications Corp. at 1-800-ORDER-BOOKS.

Enjoy,
Brad Templeton

# Chapter One
# Computer & Science Jokes

The Internet's earliest members were technology people as you might expect. That's why over ⅓ of the material in this book is comedy related to computers, computer networks, the UNIX operating system, science and mathematics. This humour, aimed at the academic, scientific and computer using audience of the net, has been a specialty of **rec.humor.funny** since its beginning.

If you're not a computer user—beware. Some of these jokes aren't going to make any sense. If you're not familiar with some of the culture and history of the Internet and USENET, some will make even less sense. Of course, they may not make sense to computer people either, but that's just part of the conspiracy.

---

## PROGRAMMING THE HARD WAY
merriam@ecst.csuchico.edu (Charles Merriam)                              chuckle, computer, original

I made this up after we hired a programmer from Hewlett-Packard.

A programmer for Hewlett-Packard went to the doctor complaining about pain in her wrists. The doctor poked and prodded her (with cold instruments) for a while and issued of a prognosis.

*"You have carpal tunnel syndrome, but it's in its early stages. You should be able to continue work, but you should give up half of your programming."*

*"Which half? Writing memos about it or attending meetings about it?"*

---

## SOFTWARE VS. SILVERWARE
Kanef@charon.arc.nasa.gov (Bob Kanefsky)                              original, computer, chuckle

*If only software dealers were as fastidious as restaurants.*

A restaurant will give me the food for free if I find one bug in it.

---

## MATH KNOWLEDGE

kaplanr@govt.shearson.com (Roger Kaplan)

laugh

Two mathematicians were having dinner in a restaurant, arguing about the average mathematical knowledge of the American public. One mathematician claimed that this average was woefully inadequate, the other maintained that it was surprisingly high.

*"I'll tell you what,"* said the cynic, *"ask that waitress a simple math question. If she gets it right, I'll pick up dinner. If not, you do."* He then excused himself to visit the men's room, and the other called the waitress over.

*"When my friend comes back,"* he told her, *"I'm going to ask you a question, and I want you to respond 'one third x cubed.' There's twenty bucks in it for you."* She agreed.

The cynic returned from the bathroom and called the waitress over. *"The food was wonderful, thank you,"* the mathematician started. *"Incidentally, do you know what the integral of x squared is?"*

The waitress looked pensive; almost pained. She looked around the room, at her feet, made gurgling noises, and finally said, *"Um, one third x cubed?"*

*So the cynic paid the check. The waitress wheeled around, walked a few paces away, looked back at the two men, and muttered under her breath, "...plus a constant."*

**:-) Your basic smiley**

## BILLYGATE

witte@cunixf.cc.columbia.edu (Breck Witte)
Columbia University Libraries Systems Office

topical, computer, smirk

Bill Gates is building a new massive mansion, most of it underground. I guess he is doing this because he doesn't want to spend another dime on Windows. Or, perhaps, he is getting ready to throw a few stones.

## WHAT LANGUAGE IS AFOOT?

bp@thedog.cis.ufl.edu (Brian Pane)                                    computer, chuckle

How to Determine Which Programming Language You're Using:

The proliferation of modern programming languages which seem to have stolen countless features from each other sometimes makes it difficult to remember which language you're using. This guide is offered as a public service to help programmers in such dilemmas.

C   You shoot yourself in the foot.

Assembly You crash the OS and overwrite the root disk. The system administrator arrives and shoots you in the foot. After a moment of contemplation, the administrator shoots himself in the foot and then hops around the room rabidly shooting at everyone in sight.

C++  You accidentally create a dozen instances of yourself and shoot them all in the foot. Providing emergency medical care is impossible since you can't tell which are bitwise copies and which are just pointing at others and saying, "that's me, over there."

Ada  If you are dumb enough to actually use this language, the United States Department of Defense will kidnap you, stand you up in front of a firing squad, and tell the soldiers, "Shoot at his feet."

Modula/2 After realizing that you can't actually accomplish anything in the language, you shoot yourself in the head.

sh, csh,etc. You can't remember the syntax for anything, so you spend five hours reading man pages before giving up. You then shoot the computer and switch to C.

Smalltalk You spend so much time playing with the graphics and windowing system that your boss shoots you in the foot, takes away your workstation, and makes you develop in COBOL on a character terminal.

APL  You hear a gunshot, and there's a hole in your foot, but you don't remember enough linear algebra to understand what the hell happened.

## MORE PROG. LANG. HELP

bobmon@iuvax.cs.indiana.edu (RAMontante)                           computer, smirk

The lovely explanation of how to identify a programming language by its effects missed a few languages. Herewith:

**FORTRAN:** You shoot yourself in each toe, iteratively, until you run out of toes, then you read in the next foot and repeat. If you run out of bullets, you continue anyway because you have no exception processing ability.

**Algol:** You shoot yourself in the foot with a musket. The musket is aesthetically fascinating, and the wound baffles the adolescent medic in the emergency room.

**COBOL:** USEing a COLT45 HANDGUN, AIM gun at LEG.FOOT, THEN place ARM.HAND.FINGER on HANDGUN.TRIGGER, and SQUEEZE. THEN return HANDGUN to HOLSTER. Check whether shoelace needs to be retied.

**BASIC:** Shoot self in foot with water pistol. On big systems, continue until entire lower body is waterlogged.

**PL/I:** You consume all available system resources, including all the offline bullets. The DataProcessing & Payroll Department doubles its size, triples its budget, acquires four new mainframes, and drops the original one on your foot.

**SNOBOL:** You grab your foot with your hand, then rewrite your hand to be a bullet. The act of shooting the original foot then changes your hand/bullet into yet another foot (a left foot).

**lisp:** You shoot yourself in the appendage which holds the gun with which you shoot yourself in the appendage which holds the gun with which you shoot yourself in the appendage which holds the gun with which you shoot yourself in the appendage which holds...

**scheme:** You shoot yourself in the appendage which holds the gun with which you shoot yourself in the appendage which holds the gun with which you shoot yourself in the appendage which holds the gun with which you shoot yourself in the appendage which holds... ..but none of the other appendages are aware of this happening.

**English:** You put your foot in your mouth, then bite it off.

## SHOOT YOURSELF IN THE FOOT YET AGAIN.

PLS@cup.portal.com

computer, chuckle

I copied the last jokes about shooting yourself in the foot in various languages to BIX. Here are their additions.

**Prolog:** You attempt to shoot yourself in the foot, but the bullet, failing to find its mark, backtracks into the gun which then explodes in your face. <BG>

**Forth:** yourself foot shoot. <akarna>

**DBase:** You squeeze the trigger, but the bullet moves so slowly that by the time your foot feels the pain you've forgotten why you shot yourself anyway. <rboatright >

**DBase IV version 1.0:** You pull the trigger, but it turns out that the gun was a poorly-designed grenade and the whole building blows up. <akarna>

**CLIPPER:** You grab a bullet, get ready to insert it in the gun so that you can shoot yourself in the foot, and discover that the gun that the bullet fits has not yet been built, but should be arriving in the mail *REAL SOON NOW*. <rboatright >

**SQL:** You cut your foot off, send it out to a service bureau and when it returns, it has a hole in it, but will no longer fit the attachment at the end of your leg. <rboatright>

**ASSEMBLY LANGUAGE:** For those who like to load their own rounds before shooting themselves in the foot. <rhsmith>

---

**:-P Nyahhh!**

---

## SCHRODINGER'S CAT

Johan Blixt <blixt@trantor.math.kth.se>

funny, true

Found in "The Guardian." (GBR)

Disregarding the metaphysical aspects of Schrodinger's cats, (Letters, April 28) I must protest at the use of (possibly live) animals for experiments such as these. I urge readers to boycott whatever product this research is leading to.

Roger Bisby, Reigate, Surrey.

## MACINTOSH JOKE

wjjordan@watdragon.UUCP (W. Jim Jordan)                                    heard it, funny
Canadian Coca-Cola Classic Consumption Centre, Waterloo, Ontario

What's the difference between a MacIntosh and an Etch-A-Sketch?

*You don't have to shake the Mac to clear the screen.*

## HUMOUROUS QUOTES FROM PROFESSORS AT UW

mathnews@watmath.waterloo.edu (Math society newsletter)                    chuckle
(The math department here at UW has a student run news/humour magazine called, appropriately
enough, mathNEWS. One of the best columns in there is the prof quotes. This is what keeps us
awake in Friday morning classes:)

*"Has anyone had problems with the computer accounts?"*
*"Yes, I don't have one."*
*"Okay, you can send mail to one of the tutors..."*

*E. D'Azevedo Computer Science 372*

*"If that makes any sense to you, you have a big problem."*

*C. Durance Computer Science 234*

*"Let's make ethanol green this afternoon."*

*R. Friesen Chemistry 124*

*"You can write a small letter to Grandma in the filename."*

*Forbes Burkowski Computer Science 454*

*"What I've done, of course, is total garbage."*

*R. Willard Pure Math 430a*

*"The algorithm to do that is extremely nasty. You might want to mug
someone with it?"*

*M. Devine Computer Science 340*

*"Is it a really good acid, or just a half-acid?"*

*R. Friesen Chemistry 124*

*"You can do this in a number of ways. IBM chose to do all of them. Why
do you find that funny?"*

*D. Taylor Computer Science 350*

"This process can check if this value is zero, and if it is, it does something child-like."

*Forbes Burkowski Computer Science 454*

"I think it is true for all n. I was just playing it safe with n=3 because I couldn't remember the proof."

*Baker Pure Math 351a*

"Now this is a totally brain damaged algorithm. Gag me with a smurfette."

*P. Buhr Computer Science 354*

"Every prof blows this. We're all going to get AIDS or something."

*J. Vanderkooy Physics 122*

"How do you find an isomorphism? You just f it. See? Graph theory is a lot of fun."

*I. Goulden Combinatorics and Optimization 230*

"You can't drink negative beer. Well, I guess you could throw up."

*Forbes Math Elective 102*

"Due to the postal strike, the assignment is extended to one week from today. I do not give out extensions without good reason."

*Forbes Burkowski Computer Science 454*

"You can bring any calculator you like to the midterm, as long as it doesn't dim the lights when you turn it on."

*Hepler Systems Design 182*

"You have to regard everything I say with suspicion - I may be trying to bullshit you, or I may just be bullshitting you inadvertently."

*J. Wainwright Mathematics 140b*

"Pascal is Pascal is Pascal is dog meat."

*M. Devine and P. Larson Computer Science 340*

"We'll call it S for cyclic."

*Gord Sinnamon Mathematics 234b*

"Karen has her own i, and she is not going to let Frank put his data into it."

*F. D. Boswell Computer Science 240*

"All that was meant to bore you shitless."

*I. Goulden Combinatorics and Optimization 230*

"The subspace W inherits the other 8 properties of V. And there aren't even any property taxes."

*J. MacKay Mathematics 134b*

"So you have this mapping P(v). So what does it mean? It means you take v and 'P' on it, right?"

*J. Baker Mathematics 234b*

"That's an engineer on his work term. He's sawing pipes, then soldering them back together again...He'll do that 10 times to make the pipe shorter."

*J. MacKay Statistics 332*

"What do I do if I am running low on my [computer] account?"
"Take out a loan."

*C. Durance Computer Science 234*

## MAIL AND FEMAIL
kcollinsthom@lion.UUCP (Kevyn Collins-Thompson)          chuckle, true, computer

One day, after I logged in to my CMS account here, I discovered that new mail was waiting for me in my reader. The lengthy message was prefaced by the heading:

"From: Mailer@<machine>: Your message could not be sent ..etc"
"Reason: Address unknown..."

Upon scanning this returned letter, I discovered that it had not been written by me at all, and that the intended recipient and sender were thousands of miles away, apparently the unfortunate victims of a random mailer screw-up. The first sentence of that letter, though, I will always remember:

"My dearest Janice: At last, we have a method of non-verbal communication which is completely private..."

## AI KOANS

ajs@hpfcajs.UUCP                                                                                      chuckle

(From sri-unix!greiner@Diablo)

A novice was trying to fix a broken Lisp machine by turning the power off and on. Knight, seeing what the student was doing spoke sternly: *"You can not fix a machine by just power-cycling it with no understanding of what is going wrong."* Knight turned the machine off and on. The machine worked.

One day a student came to Moon and said, *"I understand how to make a better garbage collector. We must keep a reference count of the pointers to each cons."* Moon patiently told the student the following story:

"One day a student came to Moon and said, *"I understand how to make a better garbage collector...*

In the days when Sussman was a novice Minsky once came to him as he sat hacking at the PDP-6. *"What are you doing?"* asked Minsky. *"I am training a randomly wired neural net to play Tic-Tac-Toe."* *"Why is the net wired randomly?"* asked Minsky. *"I do not want it to have any preconceptions of how to play."* Minsky shut his eyes. *"Why do you close your eyes?"* Sussman asked his teacher. *"So the room will be empty."* At that moment, Sussman was enlightened.

A student, in hopes of understanding the Lambda-nature, came to Greenblatt. As they spoke a Multics system hacker walked by. *"Is it true,"* asked the student, *"that PL-1 has many of the same data types as Lisp?"* Almost before the student had finished his question, Greenblatt shouted, *"FOO!"* and hit the student with a stick.

A disciple of another sect once came to Drescher as he was eating his morning meal. *"I would like to give you this personality test,"* said the outsider, *"because I want you to be happy."* Drescher took the paper that was offered him and put it into the toaster: *"I wish the toaster to be happy, too."*

A man from AI walked across the mountains to SAIL to see the Master, Knuth. When he arrived, the Master was nowhere to be found. *"Where is the wise one named Knuth?"* he asked a passing student. *"Ah,"* said the student, *"you have not heard. He has gone on a pilgrimage across the mountains to the temple of AI to seek out new disciples."* Hearing this, the man was Enlightened.

A famous Lisp Hacker noticed an Undergraduate sitting in front of a Xerox 1108, trying to edit a complex Klone network via a browser. Wanting to help, the Hacker clicked one of the nodes in the network with the mouse, and asked, *"what do you see?"* Very earnestly, the Undergraduate replied *"I see a cursor."* The Hacker then quickly pressed the boot toggle at the back of the keyboard, while simultaneously hitting the Undergraduate over the head with a thick Interlisp Manual. The Undergraduate was then Enlightened.

---

**:-& Smiley which is tongue-tied**

---

## NEW LANGUAGES
maxwell@ablnc.UUCP                                                    heard it, chuckle

(I saw a request on the net a while back that I think was referring to this article or a similar one. It is a little dated, but I think it still has some humor. My copy has no copyright notices and attributes the original to the APL SIG newsletter. I believe my copy came from a DECUS newsletter or magazine. This is a verbatim copy from my photocopy of the original.)

### Languages NOT included in the Commercial Language SIG or the Languages and Tools SIG

by
Doug Bohrer
Bohrer and Company
Near Chicago
and
Ted A. Bear
NCA Corporation
In the heart of Silicon Valley
and
A Usually Reliable Source
Digital Equipment Corporation
Somewhere in New England

**APL, BASIC, COBOL, FORTRAN, PASCAL, RPG**... these programming languages are well known and (more or less) loved throughout the computer industry. There are numerous other languages, however, that are less well known yet still have ardent devotees. In fact, these little known languages generally have the most fanatic admirers. For those who wish to know more about these obscure languages—and why they are obscure—we present the following catalogue.

C-This language was named for the grade received by its creator when he submitted it as a class project in a graduate programming class. C- is best described as a "low-level" programming language. In general, the language requires more C- statements than machine code instructions to execute a given task. In this respect it is very similar to COBOL.

**DOGO**—Developed at MIOT (Massachusetts Institute of Obedience Training). DOGO heralds a new era of computer-literate pets. DOGO commands include SIT, HEEL, STAY, PLAY_DEAD and ROLL_OVER. An innovative feature of DOGO is "puppy graphics," a small cocker spaniel that occasionally leaves deposits as it travels across the screen.

**FIFTH—FIFTH** is a precise mathematical language in which the data types refer to quantities. The data types range from CC, OUNCE, SHOT and JIGGER to FIFTH (hence the name of the language), LITER MAGNUM, and BLOTTO. Commands refer to ingredients such as CHABLIS, CHARDONNAY, CABERNET, GIN, VERMOUTH, VODKA, SCOTCH, BOURBON, CANADIAN, COORS, BUD, EVERCLEAR and WHAT_EVERS_AROUND.

The many versions of the FIFTH language reflect the sophistication and financial status of the user. Commands in the ELITE dialect include VSOP, LAFITE and WAITERS_RECOMMENDATION. The GUTTER dialect commands include THUNDERBIRD, RIPPLE and HOUSE_RED. The GUTTER dialect is a particular favorite of frustrated FORTH programmers who end up using this language.

**LAIDBACK**—This language was developed at the Marin County Center for T'ai Chi, Mellowness and Computer Programming (now defunct), as an alternative to the more intense atmosphere in nearby Silicon Valley.

The center was ideal for programmers who liked to soak in hot tubs while they worked. Unfortunately few programmers could survive there because the center outlawed Pizza and Coca-Cola in favor of Tofu and Perrier.

Many mourn the demise of LAIDBACK because of its reputation as a gentle and non-threatening language since all error messages are in lower case. For example, LAIDBACK responded to syntax errors with the message: "I hate to bother you, but i just can't relate to that. can you find the time to try it again?"

**LITHP**—This otherwise unremarkable language is distinguished by the absence of an "S" in its character set. Programmers and users must substitute "TH." LITHP is said to be useful prothething litht. This language was developed in San Francisco.

**REAGAN**—This language was also developed in California, but is now widely used in Washington D.C. It is the current subset of the international bureaucratic language known as DOUBLESPEAK. Commands include REVENUE_ENHANCEMENT, STOCKMAN, CAP_WEINBERGER, MALCOMB_BALDRIDGE, CABINET, CHOP_WOOD, LAXALT and SCENERIO. WATT and BURFORD have been removed from the commands while there is a current effort to add MEESE.

The operating system used is NEW_RIGHT and the designated memory is THE_RANCH. The compile SCENERIO is a compile with NANCY followed by a link with BONZO resulting in a SNOOZE. COMMIES (program bugs) are removed with the GRENADA command.

A REAGAN program commences with LANDSLIDE and terminates with SENILITY.

**RENE**—Named after the famous French philosopher and mathematician Rene DesCartes, RENE is a language used for artificial intelligence. The language is being developed at the Chicago Center of Machine Politics and Programming under a grant from the Jane Byrne Victory Fund. A spokesman described the language as "Just as great as dis [sic] city of ours."

The center is very pleased with progress to date. They say they have almost succeeded in getting a VAX to think. However, sources inside the organization say that each time the machine fails to think it ceases to exist.

**SARTRE**—Named after the late existential philosopher, SARTRE is an extremely unstructured language. Statements in SARTRE have no purpose; they just are. Thus SARTRE programs are left to define their own functions. SARTRE programmers tend to be boring and depressing and are no fun at parties.

**SIMPLE**—SIMPLE is the acronym for Sheer Idiot's Monopurpose Programming Linguistic Environment. This language, developed at Hanover College for Technological Misfists, was designed to make it impossible to write code with errors in it. The statements are, therefore, confined to BEGIN, END and STOP. No matter how you arrange the statements, you can't make a syntax error.

**SLOBOL**—SLOBOL is best know for the speed, or the lack of it, of the compiler. Although may compilers allow you to take a coffee break while they compile, the SLOBOL compiler allows you to travel to Columbia to pick the coffee. Forty-three programmers are known to have died of boredom sitting at their terminals while waiting for a SLOBOL program to compile.

**VALGOL**—From its modest beginnings in Southern California's San Fernando Valley, VALGOL is enjoying a dramatic surge of popularity across the industry.

VALGOL commands include REALLY, LIKE, WELL and Y*KNOW. Variables are assigned with the =LIKE and +TOTALLY operators. Other operators include the California Booleans, AX and NOWAY. Repetitions of code are handled in FOR - SURE loops.

Here is a sample program:

```
        LIKE, Y*KNOW(I MEAN)START
IF PIZZA                =LIKE BITCHEN AND
GUY                     =LIKE TUBULAR AND
VALLEY GIRL             =LIKE GRODY**MAX(FERSURE)**2
THEN

        FOR I=LIKE 1 TO OH*MAYBE 100
            DO*WAH - (DITTY**2)
            BARF(I)=TOTALLY GROSS(OUT)
        SURE

        LIKE BAG THIS PROGRAM
        REALLY
        IM*SURE
        GOTO THE MALL
```

VALGOL is characterized by its unfriendly error messages. For example, when the user makes a syntax error, the interpreter displays the message:

```
GAG ME WITH A SPOON!!
```

## THE FAMOUS ENTERPRISE / ROAD RUNNER STORY
Kee Hinckley <nazgul@apollo>                                          laugh

[Ed: By David Wald, unless somebody else steps forward ]

*. . . Let us suppose that the Enterprise is doing some sort of research mission to an unknown planet. I think the Captain's Log would be worth a look:*

CAPTAIN'S LOG, Stardate 54324.5: Starfleet Command has directed the Enterprise to do a preliminary exploration of planet—in advance of a full research team. Scanners report the atmosphere to be breathable, but are receiving confusing readings with regard to life forms. I am beaming down with a landing party composed of all our chief officers except for poor Scotty.

SUPPLEMENT: Redshirt Riley has received a head injury, apparently while exploring under a high rock shelf. He reports only hearing a loud sound and jumping before being struck. After examination by Dr. McCoy he has been judged capable of continuing duty.

SUPPLEMENT: We have encountered an alien creature on this planet. While it does not itself seem menacing, a unfortunate occurrence took place when it was present. Specifically, on my orders Lt. Sulu withdrew his phaser. The creature disappeared leaving a puff of smoke, immediately following which a loud noise was heard next to Sulu. Sulu fired, hitting Ens. Chekov. Oddly enough, although Sulu's weapon was set to stun, Chekov was also covered with a black powder similar to soot. Mr. Chekov has been sent back to the ship for examination and quarantine.

STARDATE 54326.2, Mr. Spock reporting: Tricorder readings indicate that the creature we encountered earlier is constantly moving at great speed over the surface of the planet. We have encountered the creature once again. In an attempt to slow the creature for study, I attempted to fire on it. The creature, however, appeared to move faster than the phaser beam. Regretfully, the beam struck an outcropping of rock above the Captain's head, causing it to break off and fall. Although it appears that several tons of rock fell squarely on the Captain, he was driven straight into the ground but apparently not seriously injured, though stunned. The Captain has been beamed up to Sickbay, leaving me in command of the research party.

CAPTAIN'S LOG, Stardate 54342.1: The creature is still at large on the planet's surface. While Mr. Spock continues to lead a research party I am currently at work with Mr. Scott on an Acme Pressure Cooker for our lab, for when the creature is finally apprehended.

CAPTAIN'S LOG, stardate 54342.3. The strange occurrences that have dogged the landing party since our arrival at this planet have led me to believe that the creature is in some way directly responsible for them. Mr. Chekov and I have both been declared fit for return to duty, though Dr. McCoy has entered in his medical log that he feels we should be kept under observation. Mr. Spock has constructed a device which he suspects should be able to counteract the creature's incredible speed as follows: we have placed a dish of birdseed out in the open, with several signs pointing to it. The dish is atop a cleverly concealed trap door, which will open when any weight falls on it. The creature will then travel a slide, eventually being deposited in a cage constructed of sheets of transparent aluminum. We will then be free to analyze it at our leisure. Meanwhile, I have forbidden all beaming down to the surface of the planet except on my or Mr. Spock's direct order.

CAPTAIN'S LOG, supplemental. The plan failed. The creature was indeed lured by the birdseed, as expected. It sped to the dish, consumed the bait, and sped off without setting off the trap. Mr. Spock is as puzzled as I, and has begun tests to discover the flaw in the design. I have sent out three search parties to see if we can box the creature in, one headed by Mr. Sulu, one by Mr. Chekov, and one by Sociologist Xontel.

CAPTAIN'S LOG, stardate 54342.8. Sociologist Xontel has been temporarily incapacitated. In pursuing the creature, he and his men somehow managed to cross the place where Mr. Spock's trap was set just as he completed the corrections to it. The trap was sprung, and all four of my men were suspended for a moment in mid-air, puzzled, just before they fell into the cage we constructed. We are now trying to release them with phasers, as the lock was inadvertently smashed by the impact from Sociologist Xontel's foot as he fell. I consider this a major setback. Mr. Spock considers it "fascinating."

CAPTAIN'S LOG, stardate 54343.4. In an all-out attempt to stop the creature once and for all, I have had a phaser rifle beamed down from the Enterprise. The creature has behaved in an extremely cunning manner, yet I am unsure whether this is a sign of actual intelligence. Lt. Uhura has been unsuccessful in her attempts to raise Starfleet Command. Meanwhile, Mr. Scott informs me that our dilithium crystals are deteriorating at an alarming rate. He has juryrigged a system that will prevent the decay for a time, but it is imperative that we find new crystals soon.

CAPTAIN'S LOG, SUPPLEMENTAL. Mr. Sulu reports high energy tricorder readings from an area of the planet in which the creature has not yet been sighted. He has taken a small party, including Mr. Spock, to the high-elevation spot from which the readings emanate. I have begun to analyze the creature's movements. It seems to travel consistently over a set path. Perhaps we can corner it in a tunnel it seems to pass through frequently.

CAPTAIN'S LOG, stardate 54344.7. Mr. Sulu has located a cache of ACME dilithium crystals atop a high cliff. Regretfully, while collecting them, the edge of the cliff broke off, and he and Mr. Spock plummetted several hundred feet to the ground below. Strangely enough, they both survived the fall with no more than raising a cloud of dust on impact, although they did pass the chunk of rock on the way down and end up completely buried. A rescue excavation has commenced, and they should be safe shortly.

CAPTAIN'S LOG, stardate 54344.9. Mr. Spock has beamed up to the ship with them to assist Mr. Scott in their installation, as he forsees compatibility problems. Back on the planet's surface, Mr. Chekov led seven men into the tunnel in an attempt to capture the creature in transit. A loud BEEP, BEEP was heard, and Chekov aimed the phaser rifle and commanded his men to spread out. I wish to state for the record that I would have acted similarly, and that Ensign Chekov should in no way be held responsible for the unfortunate circumstances arising from the unexpected appearance of an old Earth-style freight train. He has been beamed back up to the ship with minor injuries.

CAPTAIN'S LOG, stardate 54345.1. Dr. McCoy has beamed down with a hypo containing a mixture of kyranide, tri-ox compound, Scalosian concentrate, a theragram derivative, and some other items he found in unmarked containers in Sickbay. By injecting a small amount into each member of the landing party, I hope to be able to deal with the creature on its own high speed terms.

CAPTAIN'S LOG, supplemental. The latest experiment to deal with the strange creature has failed. As Dr. McCoy was injecting a measured dose of the compound, it abruptly appeared behind him and uttered a loud BEEP, BEEP! Dr. McCoy, understandably flustered, accidentally pressured in the entire contents of the hypo into his arm. A full security team is in pursuit of him, waiting for the effects of the drug to wear off.

CAPTAIN'S LOG, stardate 54345.2. I have ordered the landing party transported back to the ship. The new dilithium crystals have been successfully installed. On my responsibility, the ship is preparing to engage main phasers to attack the creature, which continues on its semi-erratic course across the planet's surface.

CAPTAIN'S LOG, SUPPLEMENTAL. This is a warning to all other starships that may pass this way. Do not approach this planet! The illogical events occuring here are too much to overcome with simple science. If you have heard the events transcribed in the rest of this log, you will learn that this creature is nearly undefeatable. We channelled full ship's power through the phaser banks. Theoretically, the creature should have been destroyed; however, the energies were too much strain for the ACME crystals. The full force of the phasers backlashed over the Enterprise, engulfing her completely. At first, the only noticeable effect was a complete failure of all systems save emergency gravity and life support. Then a web of black lines spread through the Enterprise's superstructure. Next, the ship began breaking up, piece by piece, falling through the atmosphere to land on the surface of the planet. When the ship had collapsed entirely, my crew was left hanging in space for a short time, and finally each of us began to fall to the planet below. We have no theories on how any of us survived, but every crewmember has reported nothing more than a sense of uneasiness, followed by the realization that they were several hundred miles up in the air, a sinking sensation, and then a gradual drop: first the feet, then the body, and finally the head, usually wearing a resigned expression of perplexity. We are attempting now to communicate with the creature in the hopes that it will prove intelligent. Perhaps we can communicate our peaceful intentions to it. Mr. Spock has constructed a crude rocket launcher from the wreckage of the ship, and with this we hope to send the recorder marker up into space, where hopefully someone will find it. Captain James T. Kirk, of the United Federation of Planets, Captain of the Starship Enterprise, recording.

```
<:| Dunce
```

## COBOL FOREVER

jbtubman@noah.arc.cdn (Jim Tubman)
Alberta Research Council, Calgary

computer, funny

Remark made by Bertrand Meyer (inventor of the Eiffel language) at a panel discussion at OOPSLA '89:

"COBOL programmers are destined to code COBOL for the rest of their lives, and thereafter."

## SELECTING A PROGRAMMING LANGUAGE

BRIAN%nuacc.bitnet@rutgers.edu (Brian Wilson)　　　　original, chuckle, heard it

### Selecting a Programming Language Made Easy

Daniel Solomon & David Rosenblueth
Department of Computer Science, University of Waterloo
Waterloo, Ontario, Canada N2L 3G1

With such a large selection of programming languages it can be difficult to choose one for a particular project. Reading the manuals to evaluate the languages is a time consuming process. On the other hand, most people already have a fairly good idea of how various automobiles compare. So in order to assist those trying to choose a language, we have prepared a chart that matches programming languages with comparable automobiles.

| | |
|---|---|
| **Assembler** | A Formula I race car. Very fast, but difficult to drive and expensive to maintain. |
| **FORTRAN II** | A Model T Ford. Once it was king of the road. |
| **FORTRAN IV** | A Model A Ford. |
| **FORTRAN 77** | A six-cylinder Ford Fairlane with standard transmission and no seat belts. |
| **COBOL** | A delivery van. It's bulky and ugly, but it does the work. |
| **BASIC** | A second-hand Rambler with a rebuilt engine and patched upholstry. Your dad bought it for you to learn to drive. You'll ditch the car as soon as you can afford a new one. |
| **PL/I** | A Cadillac convertible with automatic transmission, a two- tone paint job, white-wall tires, chrome exhaust pipes, and fuzzy dice hanging in the windshield |
| **C** | A black Firebird, the all-macho car. Comes with optional seat belts (lint) and optional fuzz buster (escape to assembler). |
| **ALGOL 60** | An Austin Mini. Boy, that's a small car. |
| **Pascal** | A Volkswagen Beetle. It's small but sturdy. Was once popular with intellectuals. |
| **Modula II** | A Volkswagen Rabbit with a trailer hitch. |
| **ALGOL 68** | An Aston Martin. An impressive car, but not just anyone can drive it. |

| | |
|---|---|
| **LISP** | An electric car. It's simple but slow. Seat belts are not available |
| **PROLOG/LUCID** | Prototype concept-cars. |
| **Maple/MACSYMA** | All-terrain vehicles. |
| **FORTH** | A go-cart. |
| **LOGO** | A kiddie's replica of a Rolls Royce. Comes with a real engine and a working horn. |
| **APL** | A double-decker bus. Its takes rows and columns of passengers to the same place all at the same time. But, it drives only in reverse gear, and is instrumented in Greek. |
| **Ada** | An army-green Mercedes-Benz staff car. Power steering, power brakes and automatic transmission are all standard. No other colors or options are available. If it's good enough for the generals, it's good enough for you. Manufacturing delays due to difficulties reading the design specification are starting to clear up. |

## COBOL PROGRAMMING ANYONE?

brad@uqcspe.oz.au (Brad Broom)
Computer Science, Queensland Uni, Australia

*funny, true, original*

Sick of writing C/Pascal/Ada? This is probably enough to make COBOL programming very attractive:

An ad in *Australian*: (copied without permission)

> BANKING EXPR NOT NECESSARY
> (4)COBOL PROGS.......To 434K++
> Low Interest Loans
> 19 Day Month

With this sort of income, banking experience would soon be obtained.
P.S. Anyone got a good COBOL textbook they'd like to part with?

## IT PAYS TO BE EXPERIENCED

groo@greybox.oz.au (P.Smith)
Dept. Computing, Bendigo CAE, Australia

*chuckle, true*

Strange job advertisement in *Age* and *Australian*:

> [. . .]
> Salary $23,999 – $23,400 depending on experience.

Plenty of incentive for experienced programmers here.

## MINI & MICRO

gm@trsvax.sq.com (George Moore)                                    sexual, chuckle

Micro was a real-time operator and a dedicated multi-user. His broadband protocol made it easy for him to interface with numerous input/output devices, even if it meant time-sharing.

One evening he arrived home just as the Sun was crashing, and had parked his Motorola 68000 in the main drive (he had missed the 5100 bus that morning), when he noticed an elegant piece of liveware admiring the daisy wheels in his garden. He though to himself, *"She looks user-friendly. I'll see if she'd like an update tonight."*

He browsed over to her casually, admiring the power of her twin 32 bit floating point processors, and inquired, *"How are you, Honeywell?"* *"Yes, I am well,"* she responded, batting her optical fibers engagingly and smoothing her console over her curvilinear functions.

Micro settled for a straight line approximation. *"I'm stand-alone tonight,"* he said. *"How about computing a vector to my base address? I'll output a byte to eat and maybe we could get offset later on."*

Mini ran a priority process for 2.6 milliseconds, then transmitted 8K, *"I've been recently dumped myself and a new page is just what I need to refresh my disk packs. I'll park my machine cycle in your background and meet you inside."* She walked off, leaving Micro admiring her solenoids and thinking, *"Wow, what a global variable! I wonder if she'd like my firmware?"*

They sat down at the process table to a top of form feed of fiche and chips and a bottle of Baudot. Mini was in conversational mode and expanded on ambiguous arguments while Micro gave occasional acknowledgements although, in reality, he was analyzing the shortest and least critical path to her entry point. He finally settled on the old line, *"Would you like to see my benchmark subroutine?"* but Mini was again one clock tick ahead.

Suddenly, she was up and stripping off her parity bits to reveal the full functionality of her operating system. *"Let's get BASIC, you RAM"* she said. Micro was loaded by this stage, but his hardware policing module had a processor of its own and was in danger of overflowing its output buffer, a hang-up that Micro had consulted his analyst about. *"Core,"* was all he could say, as she prepared to log him off.

Micro soon recovered, however, when she went down on the DEC and opened her device files to reveal her data set ready. He accessed his fully packed root device and was about to start pushing into her CPU stack, when she attempted an escape sequence.

*"No, no!"* she cried. *"You're not shielded!"*

*"Reset, baby,"* he replied. *"I've been debugged."*

*"But I haven't got my current loop enabled, and I can't support child processes,"* she protested.

*"Don't run away,"* he said. *"I'll generate an interrupt."*

*"No!"* she squealed. *"That's too error prone and I can't abort because of my design philosophy."*

But Micro was locked in by this stage and could not be turned off. Mini stopped his thrashing by introducing a voltage spike into his main supply, whereupon he fell over with a head crash and went to sleep.

*"Computers!"* she thought as she compiled herself. *"All they ever think of is hex!"*

---

**(:l Egghead**

---

## OLD ONE ABOUT A PROFESSIONAL DEBATE
edw@zps.UUCP                                                    chuckle, heard it

. . . about the doctor, engineer, and programmer who were debating what the world's oldest profession was (other than the obvious one)? The doctor said that medicine was the oldest because the Lord performed surgery in the removal of Adam's rib. The engineer countered that before that act, the Lord had performed feats of engineering by creating the earth and heavens from nothing.

The doctor conceded that the engineer was right and that engineering was indeed the oldest profession. but then the programmer interjected that programming was even older. He was chided by both the doctor and the engineer saying that engineering had to be the oldest, because before the Lord engineered the earth and heavens, there was nothing, only the Great Void, only Chaos!

The programmer simply smiled and said:

*"Where do you think the Chaos came from?"*

@:I Turban

## IT'S CHEMICAL
bobc@killer.DALLAS.TX.US (Bob Calbridge)
The Unix(R) Connection, Dallas, Texas                                    chuckle

[Ed: By Thomas Kyle of M.I.T.]

April 1, 1988: The heaviest element known to science was recently discovered by physicists at Turgid University. The element, tentatively named Administratium (Ad), has no protons or electrons, which means that its atomic number is 0. However, it does have 1 neutron, 125 assistants to the neutron, 75 vice-neutrons, and 111 assistants to the vice-neutrons. This gives it an atomic mass number of 312. The 312 particles are held together in the nucleus by a force that involves the continuous exchange of meson-like particles called memoons.

Since it has no electrons, Administratium is inert. However, it can be detected chemically because it seems to impede every reaction in which it is present. According to Dr. M. Langour, one of the discoverers of the element, a very small amount of Administratium made one reaction that normally takes less than a second take over four days.

Administratium has a half-life of approximately 3 years, at which time it does not actually decay. Instead, it undergoes a reorganization in which assistants to the neutron, vice-neutrons, and assistants to the vice-neutrons exchange places. Some studies have indicated that the atomic mass number actually increases after each reorganization.

Administratium was discovered by accident when Dr. Langour angrily resigned from the chairmanship of the physics department and dumped all of his papers into the intake hatch of the university's particle accelerator. *"Apparently, the interaction of all of those reports, grant forms, etc. with the particles in the accelerator created the new element."* Dr. Langour explained.

Research at other laboratories seems to indicate that Administratium might occur naturally in the atmosphere. According to one scientist, Administratium is most likely to be found on college and university campuses, near the best-appointed and best-maintained buildings.

## THE WORM BEFORE CHRISTMAS

bradley@m.cs.uiuc.edu (David K. Bradley)                    topical, computer, original, chuckle

"The Worm Before Christmas"
by Clement C. Morris

(a.k.a. David Bradley, Betty Cheng, Hal Render,
Greg Rogers, and Dan LaLiberte)


Twas the night before finals, and all through the lab
Not a student was sleeping, not even McNabb.
Their projects were finished, completed with care
In hopes that the grades would be easy (and fair).

The students were wired with caffeine in their veins
While visions of quals nearly drove them insane.
With piles of books and a brand new highlighter,
I had just settled down for another all nighter—

When out from our gateways arose such a clatter,
I sprang from my desk to see what was the matter;
Away to the console I flew like a flash,
And logged in as root to fend off a crash.

The windows displayed on my brand new Sun-3,
Gave oodles of info—some in 3-D.
When, what to my burning red eyes should appear
But dozens of "nobody" jobs. Oh dear!

With a blitzkrieg invasion, so virulent and firm,
I knew in a moment, it was Morris's Worm!
More rapid than eagles his processes came,
And they forked and exec'ed and they copied by name:

*"Now Dasher! Now Dancer! Now, Prancer and Vixen!*
*On Comet! On Cupid! On Donner and Blitzen!*
*To the sites in .rhosts and host.equiv*
*Now, dash away! dash away! dash away all!"*

And then in a twinkling, I heard on the phone,
The complaints of the users. (Thought I was alone!)
"The load is too high!" "I can't read my files!"
"I can't send my mail over miles and miles!"

I unplugged the net, and was turning around,
When the worm-ridden system went down with a bound.

I fretted. I frittered. I sweated. I wept.
Then finally I core dumped the worm in /tmp.

It was smart and pervasive, a right jolly old stealth,
And I laughed, when I saw it, in spite of myself.
A look at the dump of that invasive thread
Soon gave me to know we had nothing to dread.

The next day was slow with no network connections,
For we wanted no more of those pesky infections.
But in spite of the news and the noise and the clatter,
Soon all became normal, as if naught were the matter.

Then later that month while all were away,
A virus came calling and then went away.
The system then told us, when we logged in one night:
"Happy Christmas to all! (You guys aren't so bright.)"

Note: The machines dasher.cs.uiuc.edu, dancer.cs.uiuc.ed, prancer.cs.uiuc.edu, etc. have been re-named deer1, deer2, deer3, etc. so as not to confuse the already burdened students who use those machines. We regret that this poem reflects the older naming scheme and hope it does not confuse the network administrator at your site.

**I -I User is asleep**

## DATA STATEMENTS...
"Henry_Cate_III.PA"@XEROX.COM
Xerox, Sunnyvale, CA

chuckle

The primary purpose of the DATA statement is to give names to constants; instead of referring to pi as 3.141592653589793 at every appearance, the variable PI can be given that value with a DATA statement and used instead of the longer form of the constant. This also simplifies modifying the program, should the value of pi change.

—FORTRAN manual for Xerox Computers

**:'-( User is crying**

## FIELD REPLACEABLE MOUSE BALLS

gregj@microsoft.UUCP

computer, chuckle, true

ESD PRODUCT SERVICE SUPPORT SUBJECT:NEW RETAIN TIP

| | |
|---|---|
| Record number: | H031944 |
| Device: | D/T8550 |
| Model: | M |
| Hit count: | UHC00000 |
| Success count: | USC00000 |
| Publication code: | PC50 |
| Tip key: | 025 |
| Date created: | O89/02/14 |
| Date last altered: | A89/02/15 |
| Owning B.U.: | USA |

Abstract: MOUSE BALLS NOW AVAILABLE AS FRU (Field Replaceable Unit)

Text: MOUSE BALLS ARE NOW AVAILABLE AS A FRU. IF A MOUSE FAILS TO OPERATE, OR SHOULD PERFORM ERRATICALLY, IT MAY BE IN NEED OF BALL REPLACEMENT. BECAUSE OF THE DELICATE NATURE OF THIS PROCEDURE, REPLACEMENT OF MOUSE BALLS SHOULD BE ATTEMPTED BY TRAINED PERSONNEL ONLY.

BEFORE ORDERING,DETERMINE TYPE OF MOUSE BALLS REQUIRED BY EXAMINING THE UNDERSIDE OF EACH MOUSE. DOMESTIC BALLS WILL BE LARGER AND HARDER THAN FOREIGN BALLS. BALL REMOVAL PROCEDURES DIFFER, DEPENDING UPON MANUFACTURER OF THE MOUSE. FOREIGN BALLS CAN BE REPLACED USING THE POP-OFF METHOD, AND DOMESTIC BALLS REPLACED USING THE TWIST-OFF METHOD. MOUSE BALLS ARE NOT USUALLY STATIC SENSITIVE, HOWEVER, EXCESSIVE HANDLING CAN RESULT IN SUDDEN DISCHARGE. UPON COMPLETION OF BALL REPLACEMENT, THE MOUSE MAY BE USED IMMEDIATELY.

IT IS RECOMMENDED THAT EACH SERVICER HAVE A PAIR OF BALLS FOR MAINTAINING OPTIMUM CUSTOMER SATISFACTION, AND THAT ANY CUSTOMER MISSING HIS BALLS SHOULD SUSPECT LOCAL PERSONNEL OF REMOVING THESE NECESSARY FUNCTIONAL ITEMS.

P/N33F8462 — DOMESTIC MOUSE BALLS
P/N33F8461 — FOREIGN MOUSE BALLS

*This came out of an IBM service database. Of course it's referring to the rubber ball inside a computer mouse...*

## NAIVE USER STORIES

peghiny@milpnd.enet.dec.com (Bluegrass For Breakfast)          true, funny, computer

### Computer Stories from a Field Service Engineer

When I worked for a company that had a contract with 3M, 3M had asked me to write them a memo describing why we were having problems with diskette failures. I said in the memo that the disks were failing due to head crashes. *"If the customers would just clean their heads periodically, we wouldn't have these problems,"* I said in the memo. One customer responded with *"What kind of shampoo do you recommend?"*

An end-user hotline received a call about a bad software disk. They asked the customer to make a copy of the disk and mail it in to the hotline. A few days later, they received a letter with a mimeographed copy of the disk. Since it was a double-sided disk, both sides of the disk had been xeroxed.

A Computer Operator says as she is lifting an RP06 disk pack from the drive: *"Gee, how much does one of these weigh?"*

Me: *"It depends on how much data is on the disk...."*

The operator believed it.

I had a similar experience while working as a student operator at Michigan Tech. One particularly trying afternoon, the computer was merrily crashing for a number of reasons. After about four such spectacles, we broadcast that the computer would be down for the remainder of the afternoon. There was a resigned groan from the users and they began to file out of the Center, except for one comely young woman with wide blue eyes who wandered up to the counter and queried:

*"What's wrong with the computer?"*

Too tired and irritated to give her a straight answer, I looked her straight in the eye and replied: *"Broken muffler belt."*

A look of deep concern wafted into her expression as she asked: *"Oh, that's bad. Can you call Midas?"*

I work for University Computing Services answering questions about any and all aspects of computing here, and as a result I run into some truly astonishing mental densities... A few excerpts from the Helpdesk:

Caller: *"What's the name for when you're entering data into the computer?"*

HD: *"Data Entry."*

Caller: *"Thank you!"*


Overheard in a student computer lab:

Client (raising hand and waving frantically): *"The computer says 'Enter your name and press RETURN.' What do I do??"*

Lab Assistant: *"Enter your name and press RETURN."*

Client (as if a revelation has struck): *"Oh!"*


Another friend of mine in a similar situation reports having a student in the lab one day, who had to abort out of the SET PASSWORD sequence because he couldn't think of a six-letter word.

---

## AT THE PLATE

jester@jessica.stanford.edu (Perry Friedman)
Stanford University

chuckle

There are three umpires at a baseball game. One is an engineer, one is a physicist and one is a mathematician. There is a close play at home plate and all three umpires call the man out. The manager runs out of the dugout and asks each umpire why the man was called out.

The physicist says, *"He's out because I calls 'em as I sees 'em."*

The engineer says, *"He's out because I calls 'em as they are."*

The mathematician says, *"He's out because I called him out."*

---

## CHURCH AND GRAPHICS SYSTEMS

janeric@control.lth.se (Jan Eric Larsson)
Dept of Automatic Control, Lund Institute of Technology, Sweden

original, computer, smirk

Question: How does one get fresh air into a Russian church?

*Answer: One clicks on an icon, and a window opens!*

---

## AN ALTERNATE VIEW OF THE UNIVERSE

stuart@wotan.hq.ileaf.com (Stuart Freedman)                    computer, smirk

Relayed-From: Bob Starkey

**beta test**, v. To voluntarily entrust one's data, one's livelihood and one's sanity to hardware or software intended to destroy all three. In earlier days, virgins were often selected to beta test volcanos.

**bit**, n. A unit of measure applied to color. Twenty-four-bit color refers to expensive $3 color as opposed to the cheaper 25 cent, or two-bit, color that use to be available a few years ago.

**buzzword**, n. The fly in the ointment of computer literacy.

**clone**, n. 1. An exact duplicate, as in "our product is a clone of their product." 2. A shoddy, spurious copy, as in "their product is a clone of our product."

**enhance**, v. To tamper with an image, usually to its detriment.

**genlock**, n. Why he stays in the bottle.

**guru**, n. A computer owner who can read the manual.

**handshaking protocol**, n. A process employed by hostile hardware devices to initiate a terse but civil dialogue, which, in turn, is characterized by occasional misunderstanding, sulking, and name-calling.

**italic**, adj. Slanted to the right to emphasize key phrases. Unique to Western alphabets; in Eastern languages, the same phrases are often slanted to the left.

**Japan**, n. A fictional place where elves, gnomes and economic imperialists create electronic equipment and computers using black magic. It is said that in the capital city of Akihabara, the streets are paved with gold and semiconductor chips grow on low bushes from which they are harvested by the happy natives.

**kern**, v. 1. To pack type together as tightly as the kernels on an ear of corn. 2. In parts of Brooklyn and Queens, N.Y., a small, metal object used as part of the monetary system.

**modem**, adj. Up-to-date, new-fangled, as in "Thoroughly Modem Millie." An unfortunate byproduct of kerning.

**pixel**, n. A mischievous, magical spirit associated with screen displays. The computer industry has frequently borrowed from mythology: Witness the sprites in computer graphics, the demons in artificial intelligence, and the trolls in the marketing department.

**prototype, n.** First stage in the life cycle of a computer product, followed by pre-alpha, alpha, beta, release version, corrected release version, upgrade, corrected upgrade, etc. Unlike its successors, the prototype is not expected to work.

**revolutionary, adj.** Repackaged.

**Unix, N.** A computer operating system, once thought to be flabby and impotent, that now shows a surprising interest in making off with the workstation harem.

---

**8:-| Net.unix-wizards**

---

## G'DAY MATE

hirayama@sumax.UUCP (Pat Hirayama)                                      chuckle, true

(From Paul Zucker, Newsbytes News Service:)

SYDNEY, Australia (NB)— A friend of Newsbytes swears that the following is a true story:

After buying a PC from a dealer of shady shady repute, the luckless customer unpacked his new toy and plugged it in to find it Dead On Arrival.

Naturally, after checking the usual things, he called the dealer and explained his problem. First question from Deviously Evasive Dealer: *"Did you check to see whether the power was on?"*

*"Of course."*

DED: *"Did you open the cover and check whether any of the boards had shaken loose in shipping?"*

*"Of course."*

DED: *"Then why are you calling me?"*

*"Well, you sold it to me and there has to be some kind of warranty,"* pleaded the frustrated purchaser.

*"Of course there is,"* replied the DED, *"But you voided the warranty when you opened the cover."*

---

**:-8( Condescending stare**

---

## MACHINE ROOM OPERATIONS

sxdjt@acad3.fai.alaska.edu (Dean J. Tabor)
University of Alaska Fairbanks                                    computer, funny, chuckle

Recently someone called me from one of the "Out on the Floor Offices," an ethereal place rumored to exist only in hyperspace, populated by mysterious beings called Users.

She was quite frantic. She was having trouble running a program through the computer, and her message was clear enough, although rather ill-conceived: *"MY FILES ARE FULL!"*

I furrowed my brow, lit a smoke, and explained to her, *"Really now, Miss Butterman, I don't have time for this."* I slowly exhaled the menthol vapors as I stopped her process, crushing any hopes she may have had of ever again seeing that document she had spent three hours slaving over.

*"I was typing this REALLY important letter, and it HAS to be ready in an hour... there's all this stuff on my screen that I didn't type... it says something about an error, should I read it to you?"*

*"No point. Just press return."*

*"Oh my, it wants my username. Can I restart that where I left off?"*

*"Not a chance."* I drew another puff and tossed the phone aside. It occurred to me that if I had to hear one more of those whining complaint sessions, heads were going to roll. Where do you people GET this stuff? I'm going to tell you what's really going on here. Now LISTEN UP. I'm not going over this a second time:

**Computer**  The black box that does your work for you. That's all you need to know.

**Response Time**  Usually measured in nanoseconds; sometimes measured in calendar months. The general rule is: Shut up your complaining about response time.

**Hardware**  See "Computer." Again, not your concern.

**Software**  If we want you to know, we'll tell you about it, otherwise, leave us alone.

**Network**  Don't worry about it, we'll take care of it. Use it to send mail among your half-wit selves, and don't think we won't read it all. What do you think we do all day? By the way, Butterman. . . shame about your mother's pancreas.

**Data** The general rule is: Don't use any data files and if you find any, delete them before I find out about them. In fact, just stay off the computer. (See *"Response Time"*)

**System Crash** Don't ever call the system manager to tell him you think the computer is down. Don't call him to ask him when it will be up again. The more you bother him, the longer it takes.

**Downtime** Like I said, don't ask.

**Uptime** Be thankful for it, use it wisely, and get out of my face.

**Overtime** Don't be ridiculous.

**Vacation** A time during which I don't have to put up with your sniveling. Don't try calling. There's no point.

**Computer Room** Keep out, you're not invited. Don't knock on the door—don't even think about it. I broke the phone last time one of you jerks called me, and I'm not about to replace it. And keep your greasy fingers off the windows.

**My Office** The name says it all. . . it's mine; stay out.

**Your Problems** The name says it all...

**Deadlines** The general rule is: Deadlines are not acknowledged by me; they're not my responsibility. Go tell someone who cares.

**Maintenance** a) A valid reason for shutting down the system at any time.

b) Much more important than anything any of you bozos do.

c) Anything I choose to call "maintenance" is maintenance.

**Software Upgrades** Far too complex for you to comprehend. If I tell you I'm upgrading the system, just be quietly thankful. It's for your own good, even if it does mean extensive downtime during peak hours.

**Electronic Mail** I delete it before it's read, so don't bother sending any to me.

**Defaults** We like them just like they are; we chose them for a reason. Don't mess with them; consider them mandatory.

**Error Messages** I'm not interested. I'm going to kill your process anyway, so keep them to yourself.

**Killing your Process** a) Don't ever ask why.

b) Beyond your control.

c) No warnings are given.

d) The highlight of my day.

e) If you call, it's going to happen. No exceptions.

**Passwords** I reserve the right to change them without notice at any time. I choose them, and the more you bother me, the more degrading yours will be. (Example: BUTTERMAN: SNOTFACE)

**Users** a) They slow down the computer.
b) They waste my time.
c) A general nuisance.
d) Worse than that, actually.

**Software Modifications** You don't know what you want—we'll tell you what you want. It stays like it is. Period.

**Privileges** I've got them, you don't need them. Enough said.

**Priority** Mine is higher than yours, accept it. That's the reason my games run faster than your lousy accounting package (*See "Response Time"*).

**Terminals** Before calling me with a terminal problem, consider this:
a) Are you prepared to do without one for weeks?
b) Do you REALLY want your process killed?
c) Did you just trip over the cord again?
d) Of course you did.

**Disk Space** I set the quotas, you live with them. If you need more space, check "Data Files."

**Operator** I hired him and I trained him. He does what I tell him to. Usually armed; always dangerous.

**Backups** A good idea if I gave a shit, which of course I don't.

**Lunch** The only time that calling my office won't result in the killing of your process.

**Data Security** That's your problem. I'm certainly not going to lose any sleep over it. My files are locked up tight. I feel secure.

**Jiffy** Length of time it takes me to resolve your problem by killing your process.

**Eternity** Length of time it takes me to give a shit about any problem that can't be resolved by killing your process.

**Impossible** a) It can't be done (as far as you know).
b) I can't be bothered.
c) You're starting to annoy me.

**Inevitable** a) Couldn't have been avoided.
b) Not my fault (as far as you know).
c) The result of annoying me.

**Menus**     If it's not on the menu, don't ask for it. It's not available. If it is on the menu, it's probably of no use or it doesn't work. We're working on it *(See "Eternity")*.

**Utilities**     I find them quite useful, you'll find them quite inaccessible. Besides, they're not on your menu, are they? What did I tell you about that?

**Nuisance**     You.

Of course, I reserve the right to add, change, or remove anything from the above list. I'm not asking you to accept these matters without question, I'm telling you.

Now that we all know where we stand, I'm sure there'll be no future problems. If you have any questions or comments please feel free to keep them to yourself. If you feel the need for more information, I highly recommend that you ask someone else.

Sincerely,
The System Manager

P.S. The new disk quota of 30 blocks per user became effective yesterday. Anyone caught exceeding the quota will lose their accounts (this means you, Butterman!).

---

`:-I Hmmm...`

---

## PROGRAMMING PEARL

BEN@vmsa.technion.ac.il (Ben Pashkoff)
Computer Center, Technion IIT, Haifa Israel       computer, funny

This was found on a sig file on another group:

"Programming is like sex:
One mistake and you have to support for a lifetime."

---

`:D Laughter`

---

## ODE TO C
stumpf@gtenmc.gtetele.com (Jon S. Stumpf)
GTE Telecom Inc., Bothell, WA

computer, chuckle

### 0x0d2C

May your signals all trap
    May your references be bounded
All memory aligned
    Floats to ints rounded

Remember ...

Non-zero is true
    ++ adds one
Arrays start with zero
    and, NULL is for none

For octal, use zero
    0x means hex
= will set
    == means test

use - for a pointer
    a dot if its not
? : is confusing
    use them a lot

a.out is your program
    there's no U in foobar
and, char (*(*x())[])() is
    a function returning a pointer

    to an array of pointers to
    functions returning char

## BUG
spirkov@ptolemy.arc.nasa.gov (Lilly Spirkovska)

original, computer, smirk

Made this one up during my morning commute:

A license plate for a VW Bug:
FEATURE

## HEAVEN & HELL

stuart@orac.hq.ileaf.com (Stuart Freedman (x1708))          computer, chuckle

Remember, I just pass 'em on... From: io!kopf!eisen (Carl West x4449)
This came in from a friend who doesn't say where it's from:

This fellow who had worked in advertising/marketing died and, upon entering heaven, met St. Peter. St. Peter said, *"In the interest of fairness, we want to give you the option to stay here in heaven, or to go to hell. You can look around here for a few minutes, then go visit hell for a while before you decide. The catch is that your decision is final— no changing your mind."*

So, the fellow started walking around heaven; what he saw, he thought to be a bit boring. People were playing horseshoes, bridge, drinking tea. It wasn't bad, but it did look kind of slow. He mentioned this to St. Peter, and asked for his visit to hell before his decision.

Immediately, he found himself standing in front of two huge doors imprinted with "HELL." Expecting the handle to be hot, he reached gingerly for it. Surprisingly, the handle was cool to the touch. Proceeding through the doors, he found a flurry of activity. People were standing around eating, drinking, dancing—in general having a great time. The marketing fellow thought that this looked like much more fun than heaven, so he promptly returned to St. Peter and told him that he had chosen hell.

Once again, he found himself in front of the huge doors. Reaching to open the door, he scorched his hand on the blisteringly hot handle. After entering, he was faced with a wall of flame, and he could hear horrendous screaming and moaning. He stood there, incredulous. The devil walked up and asked if there was some problem. *"Yes,"* the fellow replied, *"I was just down here ten minutes ago, and it wasn't hot, and people were partying and having a great time! What happened?"*

*"Well,"* the devil replied, *"that was a demo!!"*

## MEN'S MINDS

charleen@cinnamon.ads.com (Charleen Bunjiovianna Stoner)          computer, smirk, pun

The other morning, my husband leapt out of bed, eager to finish installing the new window system on our home workstation.

*"You men,"* I sighed. *"All you ever think about is X."*

## EXTENDED SIGN-OFF MNEMONICS

tlode%nyx.uucp@nike.cair.du.edu (trygve lode)                    computer, smirk, funny

These days it's quite common for messages on social-oriented bulletin boards to end with signoffs like "Hi and hugs to everybody." In fact, this has become so popular that as much as 7.5% of the disk space on some BBS's is currently devoted to this particular comment. The International Committee for Relatively Pointless Abbreviations and Badly Misspelled Acronyms (SPUDS) has just released a new, internationally approved list of abbreviated signoffs. These include:

| | |
|---|---|
| ooo | hugs |
| xxx | kisses |
| OOO | big hugs |
| XXX | big kisses |
| oo | hugs for everybody but you |
| OO! | big, excited hugs |
| CCC | hugs for people you can't quite reach around |
| OOQ | hugging with tongue |
| xx@ | kisses and earlobe nibbling |
| zzz | snoring |
| yyy | anything that occurs between kissing and snoring |
| H | handshake |
| kkk | alternate form of "handshakes for all" |
| KKK | white robes for all |
| AAA | talk-show not-really kissing |
| [X] | kissing in the closet |
| XYZZY | a kiss that moves you |
| MMM | same as WWW, but from inversion boots |
| LLL | armwrestles for all |
| OOO~~~ | big hugs and large caterpillars for all |
| ))) | smiles for all |
| TTT | trees for all |
| jjj | gooses for all |
| JJJ | big gooses for all |
| OOOXXXYYYZZZ | this is illegal before marriage in nine states |
| OOOXXXyZZZZZ | still illegal, but generally not nearly as well received |

Remember, there is much more work to be done to codify and abbreviate excessively clear and understandable sign-off messages and replace them with efficient and incomprehensible international symbols. Please contribute money, suggestions, and chocolate to this worthy cause, and help make conversation boards a better place for assembly-language programmers.

> Thank you,
> Trygve Lode,
> General Secretary (SPUDS)

## COMPUTER SUPPORT STAFF JOKES

weltyc@sirius.cs.rpi.edu (Chris Welty)
RPI CS Labs

original, computer, funny

Q: How many Unix Support staff does it take to screw in a light bulb?

A: *Read the man page!*

Q: How many Support staff does it take to screw in a light bulb?

A: *None. The bulb was fine you just forgot to turn the switch on.*

Q: Is there a UNIX FORTRAN optimizer?

A: *Yeah, "rm \*.f"*

Q: Is there a proper procedure for asking the Support staff questions?

A: *Questions will not be answered by the Support staff unless the proper procedure is used.*

Q: How do I send electronic mail?

A: *I'm busy now, please send me e-mail.*

Q: Why do Support staff email messages always end in quotes no one understands?

A: *"The way is void" —Musashi*

Q: Is there some documentation for the "tn3270" command?

A: *It's here with a description of emacs vi-mode.*

## THE COMPUTER EXPERT'S GLOSSARY

Jeff@malibu.sedd.trw.com (Jeff Pesis)
TRW Systems Engineering Research Facility

computer, funny

**ADA:** Something you need to know the name of to be an Expert in Computing. Useful in sentences like, "We had better develop an ADA awareness."

**Bug:** An elusive creature living in a program that makes it incorrect. The activity of "debugging," or removing bugs from a program, ends when people get tired of doing it, not when the bugs are removed.

**Cache:** A very expensive part of the memory system of a computer that no one is supposed to know is there.

**Design:** What you regret not doing later on.

**Documentation:** Instructions translated from Swedish by Japanese for English speaking persons.

**Economies of scale:** The notion that bigger is better. In particular, that if you want a certain amount of computer power, it is much better to buy one biggie than a bunch of smallies. Accepted as an article of faith by people who love big machines and all that complexity. Rejected as an article of faith by those who love small machines and all those limitations.

**Hardware:** The parts of a computer system that can be kicked.

**Information Center:** A room staffed by professional computer people whose job it is to tell you why you cannot have the information you require.

**Information Processing:** What you call data processing when people are so disgusted with it they won't let it be discussed in their presence.

**Machine-independent program:** A program that will not run on any machine.

**Meeting:** An assembly of computer experts coming together to decide what person or department not represented in the room must solve the problem.

**Minicomputer:** A computer that can be afforded on the budget of a middle-level manager.

**Office Automation:** The use of computers to improve efficiency in the office by removing anyone you would want to talk with over coffee.

**On-line:** The idea that a human being should always be accessible to a computer.

**Pascal:** A programming language named after a man who would turn over in his grave if he knew about it.

**Performance:** A statement of the speed at which a computer system works. Or rather, might work under certain circumstances. Or was rumored to be working over in Jersey about a month ago.

**Priority:** A statement of the importance of a user or program. Often expressed as a relative priority, indicating that the user doesn't care when the work is completed so long as he is treated less badly than someone else.

**Quality control:** Assuring that the quality of a product does not get out of hand and add to the cost of its manufacture or design.

**Regression analysis:** Mathematical techniques for trying to understand why things are getting worse.

**Strategy:** A long-range plan whose merit cannot be evaluated until sometime after those creating it have left the organization.

**Systems programmer:** A person in sandals who has been in the elevator with the senior vice president and is ultimately responsible for a phone call you are to receive from your boss. (my favorite!)

---

`>:-< Mad`

---

## DRINKING PHILOSOPHERS

pugh@panache.cs.umd.edu (Bill Pugh)
University of Maryland, College Park

true, smirk

Sandy Murphy and Udaya Shankar, two researchers at the University of Maryland, recently received a reprint request for their article "A note on the Drinking Philosophers Problem," published in Transactions on Programming Languages and Systems.

Not too unusual, except that the request came from the Research Institute on Alcoholism in Buffalo.

---

`~~:-( Net.flame`

---

## HACK SCOREBOARD I'D LIKE TO SEE
boutell@freezer.it.udel.edu (Tom Boutell)                    funny, computer

You reached the 98th place on the top 100 list.

| No | Points | Name | Hp [max] |
|----|--------|------|----------|
| 1 | $oo^2$ | hacker-Tourist died on dungeon level 99. Hacked the source for an exponential score. killed by floating point exception. | [oo] |
| 2 | 50000000 | Stallone- Barbarian died on dungeon level 20. Tripped. | [500] |
| 3 | 20938434 (Gold) | Rockefeller-Philanthropist died on dungeon level 10. Killed by socialist kobolds. | [100] |
| 96 | 1988 | Quayle-Republican died on dungeon level 1990. Sent by Bush to handle "the black dragon thing." | [Nil] |
| 97 | 1950 | Hapless-Freshman died on dungeon level 1. Killed by newt while stuck in "caps lock." | [10] |
| 98 | 1900 | You-Undergraduate quit on dungeon level 10. Remembered exam in fifteen minutes. | 2.5 [4.0] |
| 99 | 1500 | Big_Mona-Valkyrie died on dungeon level 10. Surrounded by orcs while in the "porcelain throne room." | [200] |
| 100 | 10 | Wesley-Ensign died on bridge level. Killed by absolutely everybody. | [1] |

## EVERY WOMAN IS A 10
YOURAA@morekypr.UUCP                                    chuckle, original

Every woman's a 10. It just depends upon which base you're counting in.

**3:o[ Net.pets**

## INVOLUNTARY ATTRITION
bls@u02.svl.cdc.com (Brian Scearce)                    funny, computer

I heard that people are getting laid off at IBM. I bet they open their pay envelopes and find, "This paycheck intentionally left blank."

## EVOLUTION OF A PROGRAMMER

cs161fhn%sdcc10@ucsd.edu (Dennis Lou)                    computer, funny, original

(Okay, it's late and I'm not thinking straight, but at least it's original . . . )

### High school/Jr. High

```
10 PRINT "HELLO WORLD"
20 END
```

### First year in college

```
 program Hello(input, output);
      begin
       writeln ('Hello world');
      end
```

### Senior year in college

```
(defun hello
      (print
      (cons 'HELLO (list 'WORLD))))
```

### New professional

```
 #include <stdio.h>
main (argc,argv)
int argc;
char **argv; {
printf ("Hello World!\n");
}
```

### Seasoned pro

```
 #include <stream.h>

const int MAXLEN = 80;

class outstring;
class outstring {
      private:

      int size;
      char str[MAXLEN];

public:
      outstring() { size=0; }
      ~outstring() {size=0;}
      void print();
      void assign(char *chrs);
};
void outstring: :print() {
      int i;
```

```
        for (i=0 ; i<size ; i++)
         cout << str[i];
        cout << "\n";
    }
    void outstring: :assign(char *chrs) {
        int i;
        for (i=0; chrs[i] != '\0';i++)
         str[i] = chrs[i];
        size=i;
    }

    main (int argc, char **argv) {
        outstring string;

    string.assign("Hello World!");
    string.print();
    }
```

**Manager**
```
    /* George, I need a program to output a string
        "Hello World!"  */
```

:> What?

## MICROSLOSHED WALLS

tlode@isis.cs.du.edu (trygve lode)                          computer, funny

Microsloshed Corporation of Smoke'em, Washington introduces the most
fantabulous operating system overlay ever, a high-performance GUI
(Generally Useless Interface) that will transform your measly old
command-line driven PC into a state-of-the-art multitasking system!

MICROSLOSHED WALLS

• Microsloshed Walls frees you from the worries of incompatible
hardware—in fact, if any part of your computer is in the tiniest respect
different from an original IBM PC, Microsloshed Walls will pretend it
doesn't exist and lock up when you try to install the
drivers—automatically!

• Complicated and cumbersome command-line functions have been
replaced by simple, intuitive mouse-driven commands without confusing
options or user-burdening functionality.

• Microsloshed Walls version 3.0 is a major step forward—boldly abandoning the restraints of compatibility with either DOS or Walls 2.9 applications while not making you waste your time learning new features or capabilities.

• Conventional DOS programs are limited to a mere 640K of memory; Microsloshed Walls will use up every last byte of memory on your computer and more!

• Microsloshed Walls provides your programs with a uniform user interface so simple and easy to use that all your applications will look and act exactly the same. Whether you're using a telecommunications package or a compiler, you'll be completely unable to tell them apart!

• Several of the functions of the Microsloshed applications you've grown to love under DOS will still work some of the time under Walls and a variety of Microsloshed products are very nearly supported by Microsloshed Walls including Expell, QuirkC, QuirkBASIC, QuirkPascal, and QuirkRATFOR.

• The popular word processing program Microsloshed Wart has been fully updated and modified just for Walls, making it totally unlike Microsloshed Wart while still retaining the same name.

• Microsloshed Walls includes its own special version of QEMMMM (Quirky Extraneous Massive Memory Multi-Mangler) converting your system's extraneous memory into impacted memory which can be more efficiently wasted by Walls.

We guarantee that, when you install Microsloshed Walls on your computer, you'll kiss your old DOS prompt goodbye. In fact, after just one session with Microsloshed Walls, you may never use any of your old programs again.

*Microsloshed. Software that makes your computer obsolete.*

`:@ What?`

## TWO LIONS ESCAPE FROM THE ZOO

bahn_pr%ncsd.dnet@gte.com                                    funny, computer

>From: BUNNY: :"PALMER@TALLIS.ENET.DEC.COM"

Two lions escape from the zoo. They decide that they'd better split up, but agree to meet three months later at a given spot.

Three months go by and they meet at the appointed place. One is very skinny and the other appears very robust.

The Robust One (TRO): *What happened to you? You look terrible!*

The Skinny One (TSO): *When we split up, I went to a nearby village. All I did was to eat one small person, and the villagers got very upset. They started chasing me with guns! I've been on the run ever since and haven't had a thing to eat since then.*

TRO: *That's too bad.*

TSO: *What about you? You seem to be doing well.*

TRO: *Well, I made my way to Digital headquarters in Maynard. I've been eating a manager a week, and nobody seems to notice.*

I think this could apply to most conglomerates.

**:-( Drama**

## THREE MEN AND A CAR

mckeown@cerl.uiuc.edu (John Mckeown)                          computer, chuckle

A computer engineer, a systems analyst, and a programmer were driving down a mountain when the brakes gave out. They screamed down the mountain, gaining speed, and finally managed to grind to a halt, more by luck than anything else, just inches from a thousand foot drop to jagged rocks. They all got out of the car.

The computer engineer said, *"I think I can fix it."*

The systems analyst said, *"No, I think we should take it into town and have a specialist look at it."*

The programmer said, *"OK, but first I think we should get back in and see if it does it again."*

## ANALYSIS OF SHEEP

alanc@boulder.Colorado. EDU (ALan Craig)
University of Colorado, Boulder                     science, chuckle

An astronomer, biologist, an engineer and a mathematician were crossing the border into Scotland from England on a train when they saw a field with a black sheep in it.

The astronomer said, *"Look—all sheep on Earth are black."*

The biologist said, *"Look, in Scotland the sheep are black."*

The engineer replied, *"No, in Scotland some of the sheep are black."*

The mathematician rolled his eyes to heaven and said, very patiently, *"In Scotland, there exists at least one field, in which there is at least one sheep which is black on at least one side."*

---

**[:-) User is wearing a walkman**

---

## HOW DOES A VLSI DESIGNER PAINT A LIVING ROOM?

ark@research.att.comm                                    computer, chuckle

1. Put a paint shaker in the middle of the floor.

2. Put an open can of paint in the paint shaker.

3. Turn it on. Run out of the room very quickly. Everything in the room is now covered with paint.

4. Wait until the paint dries.

5. Cover every part of the room you really wanted painted with masking tape. Leave the floor, switch plates, etc. uncovered.

6. Put an open can of paint remover in the paint shaker.

7. Turn it on. Run out of the room very quickly. Everything not covered with masking tape is now clean again.

8. Remove the masking tape.

9. Remove the paint shaker and sludge from the floor.

---

**:-X My lips are sealed**

---

## TRUE MICROSOFT STORY
alcmist@well.UUCP (Frederick Wamsley)

true, chuckle

I once got an especially helpful reply
to a question I asked on Microsoft's on-line tech support service. I wrote
back to thank them for a complete and concise reply, and said how much
I appreciated it.

The next day I had a response:

*"We are looking into the problem and will contact you with a solution as soon as possible.*

**:.( Crying**

## THE UNIX PHILOSOPHY
huff@kuhub.cc.ukans.edu (Steve Huff)
University of Kansas Academic Computing Services

heard it, computer, chuckle

Ken Thompson has an automobile which he helped design. Unlike most
automobiles, it has neither speedometer, nor gas gauge, nor any of the
other numerous idiot lights which plague the modern driver. Rather if the
driver makes a mistake, a GIANT ? lights up in the center of the
dashboard. *"The experienced driver,"* says he, *"will usually know what's
wrong."*

Original source unknown; found on Joseph Evans' (Electrical and Computer Engineering professor
at Kansas University) door.

**:] Gleep. . .a friendly midget smiley who will gladly be your friend**

## MORE UNIX FUN
trudel@revenge.rutgers.edu

usenet, chuckle

I can't claim credit for coming up with this, but...

To give nosy people grief, create a file in your home directory called
"README"— and have the file contain the words:

README: No such file or directory

**:>) User is from an Ivy League school**

## BAAASTON

scott@clsib21.UUCP (Scott P. Herzig)
CLSI Newtonville, MA

chuckle

The bridge connecting Boston and Cambridge (Massachusetts) via Massachusetts Avenue is commonly known as the Harvard Bridge. When it was built, the state offered to name the bridge for the Cambridge school that could present the best claim for the honor. Harvard submitted an essay detailing its contributions to education in America, concluding that it deserved the honor of having a bridge leading into Cambridge named for the institution. MIT did a structural analysis of the bridge and found it so full of defects that they agreed that it should be named for Harvard.

**8-I Suspense**

## SOFTWARE LAWSUITS

tada@athena.mit.edu

computer, smirk

In the wake of the recent court victory by Lotus concerning copyright infringement, Microsoft Inc. announced today that they are suing Lotus for infringing on their lawsuit copyrights. *"We have examined the text of the Lotus lawsuits and have determined that they violate our copyright on look-and-feel lawsuits,"* a spokesman for Microsoft said. *"A lot of effort was spent developing the concept of look-and-feel lawsuits and Lotus is capitalizing on our work."* At the same time, Microsoft filed for a patent on look-and-feel lawsuits.

A federal judge granted a preliminary injunction against Lotus, preventing them from pursuing further lawsuits on the basis of copyright infringement until formal briefs could be filed by both sides. Borland stock jumped $1\frac{5}{8}$ on the news.

**:-o Surprise**

`>:-I net.startrek`

## THE STRATEGIC DEFENSE INITIATIVE (SDI/STAR WARS)

jasmerb@mist.cs.orst.edu (Bryce Jasmer)                          computer, funny

Through some clever security hole manipulation, I have been able to break into all of the government's computers and acquire the Lisp code to SDI. Here is the last page (tail-10) of it to prove that I actually have the code:

```
))))))))))))))))))))))))))))))))))))))))))))))))))))))))))))))))))))))))
))))))))))))))))))))))))))))))))))))))))))))))))))))))))))))))))))))))))))
))))))))))))))))))))))))))))))))))))))))))))))))))))))))))))))))))))))))))
))))))))))))))))))))))))))))))))))))))))))))))))))))))))))))))))))))))))))
))))))))))))))))))))))))))))))))))))))))))))))))))))))))))))))))))))))))))
))))))))))))))))))))))))))))))))))))))))))))))))))))))))))))))))))))))))))
))))))))))))))))))))))))))))))))))))))))))))))))))))))))))))))))))))))))))
))))))))))))))))))))))))))))))))))))))))))))))))))))))))))))))))))))))))))
))))))))))))))))))))))))))))))))))))))))))))))))))))))))))))))))))))))))))
))))))))))))))))))))))))))))))))))))))))))))))))))))))))))))))))))))))))))
```

`%-) User has been staring at a green screen for 15 hours straight`

## NEW PRODUCT ANNOUNCEMENT

ijd@hplb.hpl.hp.com (Ian)                                        computer, funny

I heard this from Nick Rothwell of the LFCS:

Following the success of their object oriented version of C, C++, AT&T are rumoured to be working on a similar version of Cobol. Although the working name of the project is Cobol++, the product brand name will of course respect the maturity of the marketplace. It will be called ADD_ONE_TO_COBOL.

## GENERIC JOKES

albert@harvard.edu (David Albert)                              ethnic, chuckle

I hope these aren't too offensive. Perhaps they should be encrypted?

(1) A person belonging to an ethnic group whose members are commonly considered to have certain stereotypical mannerisms met another person belonging to a different ethnic group with a different set of imputed stereotypical mannerisms. The first person acted in a manner consistent with the stereotypes associated with his ethnic group, and proceeded to make a remark which might be considered to establish conclusively his membership in that group, whereupon his companion proceeded to make a remark with a double meaning, the first meaning of which could be interpreted to indicate his agreement with his companion, but the other meaning of which serves to corroborate his membership in his particular ethnic group. The first person took offense at his remark, and reacted in a stereotypical way!

(2) Q: How many people belonging to a certain ethnic group does it take to perform a particular menial activity?

A: A finite positive integer. One to perform the activity, and the rest to behave in a manner stereotypical of their ethnic group!

**X-( User just died**

## MAYBE THIS SHOULD GO IN COMP.RISKS. . .

al@crucible.uucp (Al Evans)                              unix, chuckle, true
Quoted from *Unix World,* November 1989:

The grim reality is that every life ends with a death. Funeral homes exist to make that fact a little more tolerable. . . . UNIX can help here too. The Gordon Funeral Chapel, for instance, does much of its accounting on an AT class, multiuser machine running XENIX. . .

. . .For example, Gordon says his system has to be able to classify two kinds of customer, "at need," those who are actually deceased, and "pre-need," those who have made arrangements for funerals while still living. Moreover, the system has to be able to convert one kind of customer to the other as the need arises. . .

## NEW PLAN FOR NEWSGROUP VOTING

brad@looking.on.ca (Brad Templeton)
Looking Glass Software Ltd.

original, unrated, usenet

Relayed-by: davidbe@sco.com (The Cat in the Hat)

[I wrote this, but David sent it in—I don't do my own stuff unless other people prompt it. It was prompted by the slew of silly suggestions on how to deal with the question of whether aquariums are a science or a hobby.—*ed.*]

Here's a better idea. When a idea for a new group comes up, we should have a vote on who gets to propose it. After that is decided, we can vote on who gets to pick the names. Then we'll get a list of names, and use 'New Zealand' voting rules. Under NZ rules, (OK!) each person gets 8 votes. They use 2–4 votes on the name they like most, 1–4 votes on the second best name, and so on. In addition, you get 8 negative votes for names you don't like. In the end, the vote totals are multiplied by rand( ) and the one closest to e^sqrt(pi) is the winner.

Once a name has been decided, we vote on whether we want the group or not. At the end, we vote on whether there should be a 5 day cooling-period after the vote, and if so, the duration of the the period, if not to be five, is decided by New Zealand rules. If the group champion wishes to go to the bathroom, he or she must conduct a vote lasting 14 to 30 days to decide if it is to be #1 or #2.

Finally, if it is decided that the group is to be created, and the group champion has not yet exploded, the group champion can send a request for a newgroup to wouldnot@ncar.ucar.edu. If the people on that list like the group, they will create it. If they do, each admin can then decide, as they wish, whether to carry and/or forward the group on their own machine. But otherwise the vote is binding. (Unless a vote declares it to be non-binding.)

## TOPOLOGICAL JOKE...

smm12@cl.cam.ac.uk (Mathew)
U of Cambridge Comp Lab, UK

chuckle

Heard from a friend:

Q: Why did the chicken cross the Moebius Strip?

*A: To get to the other... um... er...*

## WHY USENET IS LIKE A PENIS

davidl@ssd.intel.com (David D. Levine)
Intel Supercomputer Systems Division

original, funny, usenet

*Reasons why Usenet is like a penis:*

It can be up or down. It's more fun when it's up, but it makes it hard to get any real work done.

In the long-distant past, its only purpose was to transmit information considered vital to the survival of the species. Some people still think that's the only thing it should be used for, but most folks today use it for fun most of the time.

It has no conscience and no memory. Left to its own devices, it will just do the same damn dumb things it did before.

It provides a way to interact with other people. Some people take this interaction very seriously, others treat it as a lark. Sometimes it's hard to tell what kind of person you're dealing with until it's too late.

If you don't apply the appropriate protective measures, it can spread viruses.

It has no brain of its own. Instead, it uses yours. If you use it too much, you'll find it becomes more and more difficult to think coherently.

We attach an importance to it that is far greater than its actual size and influence warrant.

If you're not careful what you do with it, it can get you in big trouble.

It has its own agenda. Somehow, no matter how good your intentions, it will warp your behavior. Later you may ask yourself *"why on earth did I do that?"*

Some folks have it, some don't.

Those who have it would be devastated if it were ever cut off. They think that those who don't have it are somehow inferior. They think it gives them power. They are wrong.

Those who don't have it may agree that it's a nifty toy, but think it's not worth the fuss that those who do have it make about it. Still, many of those who don't have it make about it. Still, many of those who don't have it would like to try it.

Once you've started playing with it, it's hard to stop. Some people would just play with it all day if they didn't have work to do.

## THE COMPUTER GENERATION

tact04.enet!sid@decwrl.UUCP (Sid Gordon, Digital Israel, EIS)     computer, true, chuckle

My brother claims that this morning he heard his 5-year-old and his 3-year-old in the bathroom together and eavesdropped on their conversation:

Little brother: *What do I do now?*

Big brother: *Throw the toilet paper in the toilet.*

Little brother: *Like this?*

Big brother: *Yeah.*

Little brother: *Now what?*

Big brother: *Hit "ENTER."*

Little brother: *"ENTER?"*

Big brother: *I mean "flush."*

## RE: TEASING NET.PEOPLE

todd_born@sgi.com ( todd born )
Silicon Graphics, Inc.

computer, chuckle

Attributed to Dan Bernstein

Why do tech supporters make such great lovers?

*Because they know when not to answer the phone!!*

## ANOTHER ENG/PHYS/MATH

sohrt@wasatch.UUCP (Wolfgang Sohrt)     chuckle, science

An engineer, a physicist and a mathematicians have to build a fence around a flock of sheep, using as little material as possible.

The engineer forms the flock into a circular shape and constructs a fence around it.

The physicist builds a fence with an infinite diameter and pulls it together until it fits around the flock.

The mathematicians thinks for a while, then builds a fence around himself and defines himself as being outside.

## LESSONS LEARNED FROM COMP 4

denelsbe@cs.unc.edu (Kevin Denelsbeck)                    computer, funny

I recently finished up teaching Comp 4, the computer literacy course here at UNC, during a compressed summer session. Comp 4 is an introductory class that assumes NO knowledge of computers among its students, and believe me when I say that this was often the case. The class was great fun to teach, and one of the facets that made it interesting (day-in and day-out) was the wealth of new knowledge that the students imparted to me on tests and examinations. I thought that I'd share some of these nuggets with you. My comments are in the standard C delimiters (/* and */). Your comments are encouraged. Here goes:

Bacchus invented FORTRAN. /* I knew FORTRAN was old, and that it may have been designed under the influence of alcohol, but... */

There are three kinds of program statements: sequence, repetition, and seduction.

There are two types of graphics: vector and rascal. /* Otay... */

Programming languages have specifications. /* Obviously this student has dealt with a few standards. */

Macs are compatible with each other. /* Imagine the alternative: "What's your Mac's serial number? We'll go back to the warehouse and get your software." */

Doctors use computers to create a three demential picture of a person's brain. /* Is this classic, or what? */

One kind of a hostile computer program is a Trojan.

C is a logical programming language. /* <rim shot>*/

Heuristics (from the French heure, "hour") limit the amount of time spent executing something. [When using heuristics] it shouldn't take longer than an hour to do something. /* An absolutely terrific "false cognate." */

Having the computer automatically fill in images for animation is called "spleening." /* Derivation: most likely "splines" + "tweening." */

One method of computer security is a phone line. /* She qualified it later by adding, "You have to know the number." */

Video games are examples of fault-tolerant systems.

On one test, I gave the students some abbreviations and asked them to tell me what they stood for. You won't believe the creativity of a student in a test situation. For example, one of the abbreviations was "fax," which **really** stands for "facsimile." However, various Comp 4'ers said it stood for:

> Fiber-optic Aided Xeroxing
>
> Frequency Automatic X-rays

/* and my favorite... */

> Fast A** Xeroxing

The students also had to hand in term papers, and these were rife with interesting tidbits. I've clipped a few, quoted verbatim:

"The worst thing the Mac has to offer, is that cooperative multitasking is not available to be used."

"... footnotes present an interesting problem, which may be solvable by Hypercad." /* I assume the last term is the newest rage— a free-form database for designers. */

"...Linda, a blind girl, was able to attend public school due to the aid of a speaking computer that taught her the basic fundmamentals [sic] of grammar and spelling." /* Linda may want to lend her computer out... */

"The program is manufactured by Quantel, a Silicon Valley company located in Clearwater, Florida." /* A long valley, as my roommate put it. */

"At the beginning of each season [Edwin] Moses teats himself on computerized weight machines..." /* Ouch! */

---

## ORDERS OF MAGNITUDE

dale@clam.UUCP (Dale Mensch)

computer, chuckle, original

(This occurred to me while reading an article about Microsoft stock)

I've figured out why Microsoft joined the ACE coalition, agreeing to port NT to the R4000 chipset:

Intel's 32-bit integer architecture is no longer enough to calculate Bill Gates' net worth.

---

# PROGRAMMING LANGUAGES ARE LIKE WOMEN
kkirksey@eng.auburn.edu (Kenneth B. Kirksey)          chuckle, computer, sexual stereotypes

*Warning: This list may be offensive to ardent feminists.*
by: Daniel J. Salomon, Department of Computer Science, University of Waterloo, Waterloo, Ontario, Canada  N2L 3G1

There are so many programming languages available that it can be very difficult to get to know them all well enough to pick the right one for you. On the other hand most men know what kind of woman appeals to them. So here is a handy guide for many of the popular programming languages that describes what kind of women they would be if programming languages were women.

Assembler—A female track star who holds all the world speed records. She is hard and bumpy, and so is not that pleasant to embrace. She can cook up any meal, but needs a complete and detailed recipe. She is not beautiful or educated, and speaks in monosyllables like "MOV, JUMP, INC." She has a fierce and violent temper that make her the choice of last resort.

FORTRAN—Your grey-haired grandmother. People make fun of her just because she is old, but if you take the time to listen, you can learn from her experiences and her mistakes. During her lifetime she has acquired many useful skills in sewing and cooking (subroutine libraries). That no younger women can match, so be thankful she is still around.  She has a notoriously bad temper and when angered will start yelling and throwing dishes. It was mostly her bad temper that made grandad search for another wife.

COBOL—A plump secretary. She talks far too much, and most of what she says can be ignored. She works hard and long hours, but can't handle really complicated jobs. She has a short and unpredictable temper, so no one really likes working with her. She can cook meals for a huge family, but only knows bland recipes.

BASIC—The horny divorcee that lives next door. Her specialty is seducing young boys and it seems she is always readily available for them. She teaches them many amazing things, or at least they seem amazing because it is their first experience. She is not that young herself, but because she was their first lover the boys always remember her fondly. Her cooking and sewing skills are mediocre, but largely irrelevant, it's the frolicking that the boys like. The opinion that adults have of Mrs. BASIC is varied. Shockingly, some fathers actually introduce their own sons to this immoral woman! But generally the more righteous adults try to correct the badly influenced young men by introducing them to well behaved women like Miss Pascal.

PL/I—A bordello madam. She wears silk dresses, diamonds, furs and red high heels. At one time she seemed very attractive, but now she just seems overweight and tacky. Tastes change.

C—A lady executive. An avid jogger, very healthy, and not too talkative. Is an good cook if you like spicy food. Unless you double check everything you say (through LINT) you can unleash her fierce temper. Her daughter C++ is still quite young and prone to tantrums, but it seems that she will grow up into a fine young woman of milder temper and more sophisticated character.

ALGOL 60—Your father's wartime sweetheart, petite, well proportioned, and sweet tempered. She disappeared mysteriously during the war, but your dad still talks about her shapely form and their steamy romance. He never actually tasted much of her cooking.

Pascal—A grammar school teacher, and Algol 60's younger sister. Like her sister she is petite and attractive, but very bossy. She is a good cook but only if the recipe requires no more than one pot (module).

Modula II—A high-school teacher and Pascal's daughter. Very much like her mother, but she has learned to cook with more than one pot.

ALGOL 68—Algol 60's niece. A high-society woman, well educated and terse. Few men can fully understand her when she talks, and her former lovers still discuss her mysterious personality. She is very choosy about her romances and won't take just any man as her lover. She hasn't been seen lately, and rumor has it that she died in a fall from an ivory tower.

LISP—She is an aging beatnik, who lives in a rural commune with her hippie cousins SMALLTALK and FORTH. Many men (mostly college students) who have visited the farmhouse enthusiastically praise the natural food, and perpetual love-ins that take place there. Others criticize the long cooking times, and the abnormal sexual postures (prefix and postfix). Although these women seldom have full-time jobs, when they do work, their employers praise them for their imagination, but usually not for their efficiency.

APL—A fancy caterer specializing in Greek food. She can cook delicious meals for rows and rows of tables with dozens of people at each table. She doesn't talk much, as that would just slow her work down. Few people can understand her recipes, since they are in a foreign language, and are all recorded in mirror writing.

LOGO—A grade-school art teacher. She is just the kind of teacher that you wish you had when you were young. She is shapely and patient, but not an interesting conversationalist. She can cook up delicious kiddie snacks, but not full-course meals.

LUCID & PROLOG—These clever teenagers show a new kind of cooking skill. They can cook-up fine meals without the use of recipes, working solely from a description of the desired meal (declarative cooking). Many men are fascinated by this and have already proposed marriage. Others complain that the girls work very slowly, and that often the description of the meal must be just as long as a recipe would be. It is hard to predict what these girls will be like when they are fully mature.

Ada—A WAC colonel built like an amazon. She is always setting strict rules, but if you follow them, she keeps her temper. She is quite talkative, always spouting army regulations, and using obscure military talk. You gotta love her though, because the army says so.

---

**:-) Comedy**

---

## COMPUTER SALESMEN
ciaraldi@rochester.UUCP (Mike Ciaraldi)                                        smirk

Q. What is the difference between a used-car salesman and a computer salesman?

A. The used-car salesman knows when he's lying to you!

---

## NEW PUNCHLINE TO OLD JOKE
jem@latcs1.oz.au (Joan McGalliard)
Comp Sci, La Trobe Uni, Australia                    computer, funny

Q: What's the difference between a car salesman and a computer salesman?

A: The car salesman can probably drive!

---

## CHECK DISCLAIMER FOR SOFTWARE PURCHASES

lc2b+@andrew.cmu.edu (Lawrence Curcio)                    computer, funny

Disclaimer to be used when purchasing software:

### AGREEMENT AND LIMITED WARRANTY

This check is fully warranted against physical defects and poor workmanship in its stationery. If the check is physically damaged, return it to me and I will replace or repair it at my discretion. No other warranty of any kind is made, neither express nor implied including, but not limited to, the implied warranties of Merchantability, Suitability for Purpose, and Validity of Currency. Any and all risk concerning the actual value of this check is assumed by you, the recipient. Even though I or my agents may have assured you of its worth, either verbally or in written communication, we may have had our fingers crossed, so don't come whimpering back to me if it bounces.

The money, if any, represented by this instrument remains my property. You are licensed to use it, however you are not allowed to copy the original check except for your personal records, nor are you permitted to give the money itself to anyone else. Neither may you allow any other person to use the money. Remember, you may have it in your possession, but it still belongs to me, and I'm going to call on you from time to time just to keep tabs on it.

This agreement supersedes all others between us, including the equally ridiculous one you have undoubtedly pasted on the back of your packaging, or concealed somewhere in the middle of it. The location of your version of this or any other covenant between us is irrelevant to its inapplicability here. Only this one pertains, and I really mean it. In fact, this one supersedes yours even though yours may say that it supersedes mine. Why, even if yours said it would supersede mine even if mine said it would supersede yours even if yours said. . . Oh well. You get the idea.

You may decline this agreement by returning the uncashed check to me within twenty-four hours. If you attempt to cash it, however, you have implicitly accepted these terms. You may also implicitly accept these terms by:

1) Calling my bank to inquire about the status of my account;
2) Thanking me at the conclusion of our business transaction;
3) Going to bed at the end of this or any other day; or
4) Using any toilet or rest room.

Please be advised that I have adopted a strict rubber-glue policy. Any nasty thing that your lawyers say bounces off of me and sticks back to you. Be further advised that you agree to pay my legal expenses if I decide to sue you for violating this agreement or for any other reason that might strike my fancy. Violations will be punishable by fine, imprisonment, death, any two of the above, or all three.

Thank you and have a nice day!

---

`:-# Braces`

---

## IT'S THAT TIME OF YEAR AGAIN

carey@mhuxi.UUCP (Frank Carey)
AT&T Bell Laboratories, Murray Hill, NJ

MERRY CHRISTMAS

```
better !pout !cry
better watchout
lpr why
santa claus <north pole >pole town

cat /etc/passwd >list
ncheck list
ncheck list
cat list | grep naughty  >nogiftlist
cat list | grep nice >giftlist
santa claus <north pole >town

who | grep sleeping
who | grep awake
who | grep bad || good
for (goodness sake) {
              be good
              }
```

---

`:-X  Bow tie`

---

## LA BOITE BLEUE

rennie@cs.albany.edu (William A Rennie)
Computer Science Department, SUNY at Albany, Albany, NY 12222

smirk, computer

Translated from the Memoirs of Jean Turing-VonNeuman
A minor 19th century post-impressionist programmer

I will never forget that Spring, that day. Paris had an air of revolution. The week before an exhibition of Seurat's listings had caused a sensation. In his unrelenting quest for simplicity he had reduced all of programming to three machine instructions. The resulting 6,000 line bubble sort had shocked the critics.

My own recent efforts had been received poorly. I had cut and slashed through my programs, juxtaposing blocks of code in a way that exposed the underlying intensity of the algorithm without regard to convention or syntax.

*"But it doesn't compile,"* they complained.

As if programming was about adhering to their primitive language definitions. As if it was my duty to live within the limits of their antiquated and ordinary compilers.

So it was that I came that day to La Boite Bleue, seeking solace and companionship.

La Boite Bleue was where we gathered in those days. The wine there was cheap, the tables were large and they kept a complete set of language manuals behind the bar.

As I entered I heard Henri's measured accents above the din.

*"...that complexity is not the salient characteristic of exemplary style."*

Toulouse-Lautrec was seated at a table spread with greenbar. Manet, redfaced, loomed over him.

*"Damm your recursion, Henri. Iteration, however complex, is always more efficient."*

Manet stormed away from the table in the direction of the bar. He always seemed angry at that time. Partly because his refusal to write in anything but FORTRAN isolated him from the rest of the Avant-Garde, partly because people kept confusing him with Monet.

Henri motioned to me to join him at the table.

*"Have you heard from Vincent recently?"*

We were all concerned about Van Gogh. Only a few days before he had completed an order sorting routine that required no additional memory. Unfortunately, because he had written it in C and refused, on principle, to comment his code, no one had understood a line of it. He had not taken it well.

*"No. Why?"* I replied.

*"He and Gauguin had a violent argument last night over whether a side effect should be considered output and he hasn't been seen since. I fear he may have done something ... rash."*

We were suddenly interrupted by the waitress's terrified scream. I turned in time to see something fall from the open envelope she held in her hand. Stooping to retrieve it, I was seized by a wave of revulsion as I recognized that the object in my hand, bestially torn from its accustomed place, was the mouse from Van Gogh's workstation. The waitress, who had fainted, lay in an unnoticed heap beside me.

By the evening, the incident had become the talk of Paris.

---

**:-#l Smiley with bushy moustache**

---

## PROGRAMMER'S DRINKING SONG

TLS@uvmadmin.bitnet

computer, smirk, heard it

Here's a little song that was sent to me from a colleague in Rochester, NY:

PROGRAMMER'S DRINKING SONG

> 100 little bugs in the code,
> 100 bugs in the code,
>
> fix one bug, compile it again,
> 101 little bugs in the code.
>
> 101 little bugs in the code.....
> Repeat until BUGS = 0

## MORE SCIENTIFIC TRUTH IN PRODUCT LABELS

md@marvin.hq.ileaf.com (Mark Dionne x5551)  funny, science

A Call for More Scientific Truth in Product Warning Labels
by Susan Hewitt and Edward Subitzky

As scientists and concerned citizens, we applaud the recent trend towards legislation that requires the prominent placing of warnings on products that present hazards to the general public. Yet we must also offer the cautionary thought that such warnings, however well-intentioned, merely scratch the surface of what is really necessary in this important area. This is especially true in light of the findings of 20th century physics.

We are therefore proposing that, as responsible scientists, we join together in an intensive push for new laws that will mandate the conspicuous placement of suitably informative warnings on the packaging of every product offered for sale in the United States of America. Our suggested list of warnings appears below.

WARNING: This Product Warps Space and Time in Its Vicinity.

WARNING: This Product Attracts Every Other Piece of Matter in the Universe, Including the Products of Other Manufacturers, with a Force Proportional to the Product of the Masses and Inversely Proportional to the Distance Between Them.

CAUTION: The Mass of This Product Contains the Energy Equivalent of 85 Million Tons of TNT per Net Ounce of Weight.

HANDLE WITH EXTREME CARE: This Product Contains Minute Electrically Charged Particles Moving at Velocities in Excess of Five Hundred Million Miles Per Hour.

CONSUMER NOTICE: Because of the "Uncertainty Principle," It Is Impossible for the Consumer to Find Out at the Same Time Both Precisely Where This Product Is and How Fast It Is Moving.

ADVISORY: There is an Extremely Small but Nonzero Chance That, Through a Process Know as "Tunneling," This Product May Spontaneously Disappear from Its Present Location and Reappear at Any Random Place in the Universe, Including Your Neighbor's Domicile. The Manufacturer Will Not Be Responsible for Any Damages or Inconvenience That May Result.

READ THIS BEFORE OPENING PACKAGE: According to Certain Suggested Versions of the Grand Unified Theory, the Primary Particles Constituting this Product May Decay to Nothingness Within the Next Four Hundred Million Years.

THIS IS A 100% MATTER PRODUCT: In the Unlikely Event That This Merchandise Should Contact Antimatter in Any Form, a Catastrophic Explosion Will Result.

PUBLIC NOTICE AS REQUIRED BY LAW: Any Use of This Product, in Any Manner Whatsoever, Will Increase the Amount of Disorder in the Universe. Although No Liability Is Implied Herein, the Consumer Is Warned That This Process Will Ultimately Lead to the Heat Death of the Universe.

NOTE: The Most Fundamental Particles in This Product Are Held Together by a "Gluing" Force About Which Little is Currently Known and Whose Adhesive Power Can Therefore Not Be Permanently Guaranteed.

ATTENTION: Despite Any Other Listing of Product Contents Found Hereon, the Consumer is Advised That, in Actuality, This Product Consists Of 99.9999999999% Empty Space.

NEW GRAND UNIFIED THEORY DISCLAIMER: The Manufacturer May Technically Be Entitled to Claim That This Product Is Ten-Dimensional. However, the Consumer Is Reminded That This Confers No Legal Rights Above and Beyond Those Applicable to Three-Dimensional Objects, Since the Seven New Dimensions Are "Rolled Up" into Such a Small "Area" That They Cannot Be Detected.

PLEASE NOTE: Some Quantum Physics Theories Suggest That When the Consumer Is Not Directly Observing This Product, It May Cease to Exist or Will Exist Only in a Vague and Undetermined State.

COMPONENT EQUIVALENCY NOTICE: The Subatomic Particles (Electrons, Protons, etc.) Comprising This Product Are Exactly the Same in Every Measurable Respect as Those Used in the Products of Other Manufacturers, and No Claim to the Contrary May Legitimately Be Expressed or Implied.

HEALTH WARNING: Care Should Be Taken When Lifting This Product, Since Its Mass, and Thus Its Weight, Is Dependent on Its Velocity Relative to the User.

IMPORTANT NOTICE TO PURCHASERS: The Entire Physical Universe, Including This Product, May One Day Collapse Back into an Infinitesimally Small Space. Should Another Universe Subsequently Re-emerge, the Existence of This Product in That Universe Cannot Be Guaranteed.

## OBSCURE PHYSICS JOKE.
nweaver@ocf.berkeley.edu (Nicholas Weaver)                    chuckle, science

From a friend of mine: Eric.

Wanted poster in post office in physics land:

Wanted
$10,000 reward.
Schroedinger's Cat.
Dead or Alive

## POOR GREAT OLD MAN
entropy@pawl.rpi.edu (Mark-Jason Dominus)                    science, chuckle

Paul Erdos, currently most prolific mathematician in history, is always making jokes about how old he is. (He says, for example, that he is two and a half billion years old, because in his youth the age of the Earth was known to be two billion years and now it is known to be 4.5 billion years.)

He observed one day that the audiences at his talks had been getting larger and larger, to the point where they filled halls so big that his old and feeble voice could not be heard. Erdos speculated as to the cause of this.

*"I think,"* he said, *"it must be that everyone wants to be able to say 'I remember Erdos; why, I even attended his last lecture!'"*

`:-% Smiley banker`

## FERMAT'S LAST FLIGHT
msw@unix.cis.pitt.edu (Matt S Wartell)                    chuckle, mathematics

Taken from a post by Steve Simmons (scs@iti.org) in alt.folklore.computers:

Some famous mathematician was to give a keynote speech at a conference. Asked for an advance summary, he said he would present a proof of Fermat's Last Theorem— but they should keep it under their hats. When he arrived, though, he spoke on a much more prosaic topic. Afterwards the conference organizers asked why he said he'd talk about the theorem and then didn't. He replied this was his standard practice, just in case he was killed on the way to the conference.

## EMILY POSTNEWS

brad@looking.UUCP (Brad Templeton)
Looking Glass Software Ltd.

original, laugh

### Dear Emily Postnews

Emily Postnews, foremost authority on proper net behaviour, gives her advice on how to act on the net.

**Dear Miss Postnews:** How long should my signature be?

A: Dear Verbose: Please try and make your signature as long as you can. It's much more important than your article, of course, so try and have more lines of signature than actual text.

Try and include a large graphic made of ASCII characters, plus lots of cute quotes and slogans. People will never tire of reading these pearls of wisdom again and again, and you will soon become personally associated with the joy each reader feels at seeing yet another delightful repeat of your signature.

Be sure as well to include a complete map of USENET with each signature, to show how anybody can get mail to you from any site in the world. Be sure to include ARPA gateways as well. Also tell people on your own site how to mail to you.

Aside from your reply address, include your full name, company and organization. It's just common courtesy—after all, in some newsreaders people have to type an entire keystroke to go back to the top of your article to see this information in the header.

By all means include your phone number and street address in every single article. People are always responding to usenet articles with phone calls and letters. It would be silly to go to the extra trouble of including this information only in articles that need a response by conventional channels!

**Dear Emily:** Today I posted an article and forgot to include my signature. What should I do? — forgetful@myvax

A: Dear Forgetful: Rush to your terminal right away and post an article that says, " Oops, I forgot to post my signature with that last article. Here it is."

Since most people will have forgotten your earlier article, (particularly since it dared to be so boring as to not have a nice, juicy signature) this will remind them of it. Besides, people care much more about the signature anyway. See the previous letter for more important details.

Also, be sure to include your signature TWICE in each article. That way you're sure people will read it.

**Dear Ms. Postnews:** I couldn't get mail through to somebody on another site. What should I do?— eager@beaver.dam

A: Dear Eager: No problem, just post your message to a group that a lot of people read. Say, " This is for John Smith. I couldn't get mail through so I'm posting it. All others please ignore."

This way tens of thousands of people will spend a few seconds scanning over and ignoring your article, using up over 16 man-hours their collective time, but you will be saved the terrible trouble of checking through usenet maps or looking for alternate routes. Just think, if you couldn't distribute your message to 9000 other computers, you might actually have to (gasp) call directory assistance for 60 cents, or even phone the person. This can cost as much as a few DOLLARS (!) for a 5 minute call!

And certainly it's better to spend 10 to 20 dollars of other people's money distributing the message then for you to have to waste $9 on an overnight letter, or even 25 cents on a stamp!

Don't forget. The world will end if your message doesn't get through, so post it as many places as you can.

Q: What about a test message?

A: It is important, when testing, to test the entire net. Never test merely a subnet distribution when the whole net can be done. Also put " Please ignore" on your test messages, since we all know that everybody always skips a message with a line like that. Don't use a subject like "My sex is female but I demand to be addressed as male," because such articles are read in depth by all USEnauts.

Q: Somebody just posted that Roman Polanski directed Star Wars. What should I do?

A: Post the correct answer at once! We can't have people go on believing that! Very good of you to spot this. You'll probably be the only one to make the correction, so post as soon as you can. No time to lose, so certainly don't wait a day, or check to see if somebody else has made the correction.

And it's not good enough to send the message by mail. Since you're the only one who really knows that it was Francis Coppola, you have to inform the whole net right away!

Q: I read an article that said, "Reply by mail, I'll summarize." What should I do?— weemba@brahms

A: Post your response to the whole net. That request applies only to dumb people who don't have something interesting to say. Your postings are much more worthwhile than other people's, so it would be a waste to reply by mail.

Q: I collected replies to an article I wrote, and now it's time to summarize. What should I do?

A: Simply concatenate all the articles together into a big file and post that. On USENET, this is known as a summary. It lets people read all the replies without annoying newsreaders getting in the way.

Q: I saw a long article that I wish to rebut carefully, what should I do?

A: Include the entire text with your article, and include your comments between the lines. Be sure to post, and not mail, even though your article looks like a reply to the original. Everybody loves to read those long point-by-point debates, especially when they evolve into name-calling and lots of " Is too!" — " Is not!" — " Is too, twizot!" exchanges.

Q: How can I choose what groups to post in?

A: Pick as many as you can, so that you get the widest audience. After all, the net exists to give you an audience. Ignore those who suggest you should only use groups where you think the article is highly appropriate. Pick all groups where anybody might even be slightly interested.

Always make sure followups go to all the groups. In the rare event that you post a followup which contains something original, make sure you expand the list of groups. Never include a "Followup-to:" line in the header, since some people might miss part of the valuable discussion in the fringe groups.

Q: How about an example?

A: Ok. Let's say you want to report that Gretzky has been traded from the Oilers to the Kings. Now right away you might think rec.sport.hockey would be enough. WRONG. Many more people might be interested. This is a big trade! Since it's a NEWS article, it belongs in the news.* hierarchy as well. If you are a news admin, or there is one on your machine, try news.admin. If not, use news.misc.

The Oilers are probably interested in geology, so try sci.physics. He is a big star, so post to sci.astro, and sci.space because they are also interested in stars. Next, his name is Polish sounding. So post to soc.culture.polish. But that group doesn't exist, so cross-post to news.groups suggesting it should be created. With this many groups of interest, your article will be quite bizarre, so post to talk.bizarre as well. (And post to comp.std.mumps, since they hardly get any articles there.)

You may also find it is more fun to post the article once in each group. If you list all the newsgroups in the same article, some newsreaders will only show the the article to the reader once! Don't tolerate this.


Q: How do I create a newsgroup?

A: The easiest way goes something like " inews -C newgroup," and while that will stir up lots of conversation about your new newsgroup, it might not be enough.

First post a message in news.groups describing the group. Hold discussion for a short while, and then ask for a vote. Collect votes for 30 days. Every few days post a long summary of all the votes so that people can complain about bad mailers and double votes. It means you'll be more popular and get lots of mail. At the end of thirty days if you have 100 more yes votes than no votes you may create the group.

No matter what the group, it is not necessary to get the approval of admins at backbone sites. They will be happy to create any group if it passes the above test.

To liven up discussion, choose a good cross-match for your hierarchy and group. For example, comp.race.formula1 or soc.vlsi.design would be good group names. If you want your group created quickly, include an interesting word like " sex" or " bible."


Q: I cant spell worth a dam. I hope your going too tell me what to do?

A: Don't worry about how your articles look. Remember it's the message that counts, not the way it's presented. Ignore the fact that sloppy spelling in a purely written forum sends out the same silent messages that soiled clothing would when addressing an audience.

Q: How should I pick a subject for my articles?

A: Keep it short and meaningless. That way people will be forced to actually read your article to find out what's in it. This means a bigger audience for you, and we all know that's what the net is for. If you do a followup, be sure and keep the same subject, even if it's totally meaningless and not part of the same discussion. If you don't, you won't catch all the people who are looking for stuff on the original topic, and that means less audience for you.

Q: What sort of tone should I take in my article?

A: Be as outrageous as possible. If you don't say outlandish things, and fill your article with libelous insults of net people, you may not stick out enough in the flood of articles to get a response. The more insane your posting looks, the more likely it is that you'll get lots of followups. The net is here, after all, so that you can get lots of attention.

If your article is polite, reasoned and to the point, you may only get mailed replies. Yuck!

Q: The posting software suggested I had too long a signature and too many lines of included text in my article. What's the best course?

A: Such restrictions were put in the software for no reason at all, so don't even try to figure out why they might apply to your article. Turns out most people search the net to find nice articles that consist of the complete text of an earlier article plus a few lines.

In order to help these people, fill your article with dummy original lines to get past the restrictions. Everybody will thank you for it.

For your signature, I know it's tough, but you will have to read it in with the editor. Do this twice to make sure it's firmly in there.

Q: They just announced on the radio that Dan Quayle was picked as the Republican V.P. candidate. Should I post?

A: Of course. The net can reach people in as few as 3 to 5 days. It's the perfect way to inform people about such news events long after the broadcast networks have covered them. As you are probably the only person to have heard the news on the radio, be sure to post as soon as you can.

Q: I have this great joke. You see, these three strings walk into a bar...

A: Oh dear. Don't spoil it for me. Submit it to rec.humor, and post it to the moderator of rec.humor.funny at the same time. I'm sure he's never seen that joke, and I know he loves to have jokes sent to rec.humor and rec.humor.funny at the same time.

Q: What about other important questions? How should I know when to post?

A: Always post them. It would be a big waste of your time to find a knowledgeable user in one of the groups and ask through private mail if the topic has already come up. Much easier to bother thousands of people with the same question. And never bother checking at the library. What do they know?

Q: What is the measure of a worthwhile group?

A: Why, it's Volume, Volume, Volume. Any group that has lots of noise in it must be good. Remember, the higher the volume of material in a group, the higher percentage of useful, factual and insightful articles you will find. In fact, if a group can't demonstrate a high enough volume, it should be deleted from the net.

Q: What does foobar stand for?

A: It stands for you, dear.

Q: Emily, how can I put out my billboard on the information superhighway?

A: The best way to do it is to perform a spam. It's called that because everybody loves it as much as the customer in the Monty Python "Spam" sketch loves his spam.

The best way to do this is to find some naive programmer and ask it to write a script that posts your message to every newsgroup. You'll start by getting as big a list of newsgroups as you can find. The members of USENET, hoping to see your ad, have prepared these lists just for you. It doesn't really matter what your product is. If people on the net might use it, they'll be happy to read about it in every group.

Now create a message promoting yourself. Be bold, be daring, and be sure to provide info on how to contact you in ways that people on the net can't shut off. (More on that later.)

Because the reaction is going to be so overwhelming, be sure to take the following steps:

a) Unlist your phone number. The networking public is going to want to contact you so much to talk about your product or service that they'll even try to call you at home. If they get your home phone or address, they'll be sure to share it with all the other people seeking to send you their admiration, and your fame may prove too much. You want business, of course, but do you want to take orders all night?

b) Get an account with some other Internet account providers. For reasons not quite certain, your provider probably has a clause in their contract with you saying not to do this. Even if they don't, they will probably delete your account a few hours after you announce your product, so be sure to get other accounts under assumed names so you can follow what's going on. This is the reason that expecting E-mail replies to your ad won't work.

c) Be sure you've lead a clean life. You and your product are going to become as famous as Gary Hart and O.J. Simpson! But, as you know, such fame has its downsides, as your eager fans research every tawdry episode from your past history. So be sure there are no skeletons in your closet. (Unless your product is skeletons!)

d) Due to the Brady Bill, you may want to file your firearms acquisition permit a few days in advance of your ad. Soon you're going to be rich, and you'll need to protect that wealth.

e) Load plenty of fax paper in your fax machine. Hire extra staff to load the rolls. There may be orders in all the faxes you will get.

f) Resign any memberships you may have in any professional associations you may have joined relating to your business that might have something as pesky as a code of ethics. Why put them through the trouble of handling all the calls from your adoring fans, looking for somebody to talk with about you.

Ok, now you're ready. Unleash the posting program. Have it send your message once to every group. There are thousands. Now picture in your mind the prospective customer. She starts her day, perhaps, reading a group about her hobby. And right there is your ad! The title is curious so she reads it. Your name is now inserted into her mind—you've got mindshare. It's true your product didn't have anything to do with her hobby, but the net is there to find customers for you, not for people to share their thoughts.

Then she goes to her next group, perhaps about her brand of computer. There's your ad again! You've sneaked into the great demographics of the high-tech world. As she goes on, she sees your ad again and again. Imagine her joy as she sees your now familiar headline everywhere she goes. "Wow, they must be really big and important," she'll think. "They're as famous as IBM." Soon that joy will be so much that she'll be ready to buy, buy, buy.

Now comes the bad news. USENET is unreliable, and postings don't always work. So, for unknown reasons, a few hours after you make your postings they will all have disappeared. Normally you would just post them again, but by this time your Internet mail access will have been deleted, as I said above, so you'll have to just sit back and bask in the adulation and orders. There is a theory that some people, who don't like your ad, will have a smarter program than your posting program root around the net and stamp it out, but I hardly think it's likely anybody would do that.

There will be some people annoyed, it's true. But the net has at least 10 million people on it, and you'll probably only really annoy perhaps 3 to 4 million of them—a minority!

Others who have tried this have reported not only that a mere minority show displeasure, but that vast numbers of people take the time to send back inquiries and orders just so you can have more to read. Unfortunately, they rarely actually pay. Some theorize that those in the vocal minority who don't like you are sending in pretend positive responses, to waste your time. Who would bother to do that? Perhaps just 1% out of the 3 to 4 million annoyed people, at most. That shouldn't bother you too much. A similar percentage may try to phone you, or fax you, or send bricks postage due, or subscribe you to magazines. Ignore them. They're just 40,000 or so of the lunatic fringe, communist element you find on the net. They're just upset because you're making money and they're not. In fact, suckers that they are, they actually ended up paying to transmit your ad everywhere. Learn to ignore them. (That's not advice, it's just something you'll have to do.)

Now at this point you probably have to stop answering your phone, but keep those faxes coming in, and of course get ready for the mail. If you ever do get to see some of the E-mail you got sent—wow, what a flood!

When it settles a bit, threaten to sue anybody who didn't like you. That should put some fear of God into them. They should have known better than to build a system so open. Sure, they built the network as a cooperative effort, but if they didn't want your ads, why didn't they put in protections against them or enact laws to stop them? What you did was probably legal, so what's their complaint? They're like people who leave their keys in their cars and whine when they get stolen. Really, like they didn't deserve it. They just don't see the wonderful new purpose to which their network can be put, to help small, exciting firms like yours get famous. That's the American dream, after all, and you're living it, or will, when the time comes to come back out of your bunker and reconnect your phones.

---

**8-# Death**

---

## CLASSIFICATIONS OF NEWS READERS

geoff@ism780c.UUCP (Geoff Kimbrough)

INTERACTIVE Systems Corporation, Santa Monica, California                    smirk

## HOW TO IDENTIFY NEWS READERS

BEGINNER:

- Thinks rn is a typo.
- Posts empty articles.
- Wonders what '@' means.
- Accidently sends (empty) mail messages to other readers.

NOVICE:

- Knows how to read news, but seldom does, since s/he hasn't learned how to (un)subscribe to a subject.
- Posts the programmer-lightbulb joke to soc.women.
- Tries to post his/her KILL files.
- Posts articles asking what ':-)' means, and misspells it.
- Wonders why people go to all the trouble of typing in other people's articles with all those silly ">"s.

USER:

- Knows how to post followups, but uses ed to do so.
- Posts articles asking what 'SO', 'BTW', and 'MOTOS' mean.
- Has heard of KILL files, but doesn't know what they are.
- Has worn out the 'n' key.
- Still reads rec.humor

## KNOWLEDGEABLE USER:

- Knows about .signature files, but sometimes includes them twice.
- Posts flames to net.announce.newusers.
- Uses KILL files, but only on "Subject:" lines.
- Has learned to edit the "followups to:" line.
- Can save a rot13'd joke, and read it later.

## EXPERT:

- Knows how to post anonymously, from nonexistent sites.
- Posts flames about users of "notes."
- Has 0.1 megabytes of KILL files, and 5 megabytes of mail.
- Is known by name at virtually all news sites.
- Knows how to post rot13'd jokes, and can read them without saving and exiting.

## HACKER:

- Knows how to create new newsgroups.
- Has modified local version of vnews to allow longer postings.
- Uses rmgroup instead of KILL files.
- Knows how to send mail through the ARPANET.
- Can read rot13'd text without unrotating it.

## GURU:

- Has private database of alternate paths to all sites.
- Has caused at least one newsgroup to be eliminated due to low signal/noise.
- Name appears in over 1000 KILL files (at other sites).
- Uses undocumented features of rn.
- Moderates at least one newsgroup.

## WIZARD:

- Thinks rn is a typo.

---

**8:-) User is a wizard**

---

## MONTY PYTHON JOKE FOR UNIX WEENIES!

mjd@saul.cis.upenn.edu (Mark-Jason Dominus)
Martin Bormann's Cranial Splints

unix, chuckle

Stop! Whoever crosseth the bridge of Death, must answer first these questions three, ere the other side he see:

*"What is your name?"*

*"Sir Brian of Bell."*

*"What is your quest?"*

*"I seek the Holy Grail."*

*"What are four lowercase letters that are not legal flag arguments to the Berkeley UNIX version of 'ls'?"*

*"I, er.... AIIIEEEEEE!"*

## WHO'S THERE?

john@chance.UUCP (John R MacMillan)

original, unix, chuckle

Modern UNIXes have no sense of humour. I tried typing "nawk nawk" and it just sat there.

## AN ANALOGY OF OPERATING SYSTEMS, FROM HUNZEKER

vixie@decwrl.UUCP (Paul A Vixie)

computer, chuckle

Relayed-From: hall@wsl.dec.com (Jon "Maddog" Hall)

VMS is like a Soviet railroad train. It's basically industrial-strength, but when you look at it closely, everything's a little more shabby than you might like. It gets the job done, but there's no grace to it.

The Mac operating system is like the monorail at Disney World. It's kind of spectacular and fun, but it doesn't go much of anywhere. Still, the kids like it.

Unix is like the maritime transit system in an impoverished country. The ferryboats are dangerous as hell, offer no protection from the weather and leak like sieves. Every monsoon season a couple of them capsize and drown all the passengers, but people still line up for them and crowd aboard.

---

**:-S User just made an incoherent statement**

---

## GODLESS DEVIL-WORSHIPING EVIL COMPUTERS

karl@ima.ima.isc.com (Karl Heuer)                              funny, unix

Resent-From: ksr!warren@harvard.harvard.edu (If you don't understand the T-shirt image, look at your copy of "The Design and Implementation of the 4.3BSD UNIX Operating System" by Leffler, et. al.)

Resent-From: Charles Forsythe <convex!forsythe@uxc.cso.uiuc.edu>

This was sent to me by Linda Branagan—Convex doc. writer and Connie Dobbs look-alike. I think it's an excellent illustration of why "Bob" began his mission in Dallas.

The following is a true story.

Last week I walked into a local "home style cookin' restaurant/watering hole" to pick up a take out order. I spoke briefly to the waitress behind the counter, who told me my order would be done in a few minutes.

So, while I was busy gazing at the farm implements hanging on the walls, I was approached by two, uh, um... well, let's call them "natives." These guys might just be the original Texas rednecks—complete with ten-gallon hats, snakeskin boots and the pervasive odor of cheap beer and whiskey.

"*Pardon us, ma'am. Mind of we ask you a question?*"

Well, people keep telling me that Texans are real friendly, so I nodded.

"*Are you a Satanist?*"

Well, at least they didn't ask me if I liked to party.

"*Uh, no, I can't say that I am.*"

"*Gee ma'am. Are you sure about that?*" they asked.

I put on my biggest, brightest Dallas Cowboys cheerleader smile and said, "*No, I'm positive. The closest I've ever come to Satanism is watching Geraldo.*"

"*Hmm. Interesting. See, we was just wondering why it is you have the lord of darkness on your chest there.*"

I was this close to slapping one of them and causing a scene—then I stopped and noticed the T-shirt I happened to be wearing that day. Sure enough, it had a picture of a small, devilish looking creature that has for quite some time now been associated with a certain operating system. In this particular representation, the creature was wearing sneakers.

They continued: "*See, ma'am, we don't exactly appreciate it when people show off pictures of the devil. Especially when he's lookin' so friendly.*"

These idiots sounded terrifyingly serious.

Me: *"Oh, well, see, this isn't really the devil, it's just, well, it's sort of a mascot."*

Native: *"And what kind of football team has the devil as a mascot?"*

Me: *"Oh, it's not a team. It's an operating—uh, a kind of computer."*

I figured that an ATM machine was about as much technology as these guys could handle, and I knew that if I so much as uttered the word "unix" I would only make things worse.

Native: *"Where does this satanical computer come from?"*

Me: *"California. And there's nothing satanical about it really."*

Somewhere along the line here, the waitress has noticed my predicament—but these guys probably outweighed her by 600 pounds, so all she did was look at me sympathetically and run off into the kitchen.

Native: *"Ma'am, I think you're lying. And we'd appreciate it if you'd leave the premises now."*

Fortunately, the waitress returned that very instant with my order, and they agreed that it would be okay for me to actually pay for my food before I left. While I was at the cash register, they amused themselves by talking to each other.

Native #1: *"Do you think the police know about these devil computers?"*

Native #2: *"If they come from California, then the FBI oughta know about 'em."*

They escorted me to the door. I tried one last time: *"You're really blowing this all out of proportion. A lot of people use this 'kind of computers.' Universities, researchers, businesses. They're actually very useful."*

Big, big, BIG mistake. I should have guessed at what came next.

Native: *"Does the government use these devil computers?"*

Me: *"Yes."*

Another BIG boo-boo.

Native: *"And does the government pay for 'em? With our tax dollars?"*

I decided that it was time to jump ship.

Me: *"No. Nope. Not at all. You're tax dollars never entered the picture at all. I promise. No sir, not a penny. Our good Christian congressmen would never let something like that happen. Nope. Never. Bye."*

Texas. What a country.

**:- Male**

## HIGH PRICE COMPUTER
sdh@flash.bellcore.com (Stephen D. Hawley)        true, funny, racial stereotypes, computer

I recently purchased a $13 Z80 computer from Edmond Scientific (from the inventor's room). Here is an excerpt from the manual (translated from Chinese):

EVERY PROGRAM STARTS OFF WITH BUGS.

Many programs end up with bugs as well. There are two corollaries to this: first, you must test all your programs straight away; & second, there's no point in losing your temper every time they don't work. The general plan can be illustrated with this algorithm: (translated from flowchart)

```
        — Start
        — Write program with as few bugs as possible
  loop
                — test the program
                if ( program works perfectly )
                done;
  else
                — keep your hair on
                — Find the bugs
                — Fix them, introducing as few new ones as possible.
                endif
  endloop
```

**>- Female**

## ELECTRONIC LOVERS
hobson@header.enet.dec.com (Hobson's Choice)        computer, sexual, smirk

Q. Why do computer scientists make such lousy lovers?

*A. Cause they always want to do the job faster than before.*
*And when they do, they say performance has improved.*

## COVER ME

yuri@sq.com (Yuri Rubinsky)                                   computer, chuckle

After I stopped by this company's booth at the recent CD-ROM conference, the following letter arrived here from a major CPU manufacturer. . .

Dear Mr. Rubinsky:

Thank you for your [company name] literature order.

We are sorry, but the following items that you have requested are currently on backorder:

| PRODUCT CODE | DESCRIPTION | EXPECTED ARRIVAL DATE |
|---|---|---|
| T217 | Dear Customer Cover Letter | Four Weeks |

Your order will be filled at the earliest possible date. In the meantime, your patience in regard to this matter is greatly appreciated.

Please feel free to call our Literature Distribution Center at [800-number]. Our operators will be happy to help you place an order for any additional literature, or refer you to your nearest [company name] sales office to help you with any technical questions regarding our products. If you call to check the status of your order, please reference your order #[number].

Again, thank you for your order, and we hope to be of service to you in the future.

Sincerely,

[empty space here]

[company name] Literature Distribution Center

*Curiously, one week earlier I received the literature I had requested—without a cover letter.*

;-) Wink

## COMPUTER CONSULTANTS

R.POLLAND@genie.com (JOKE BOY)                                   computer, chuckle

Man talking to prostitute: *"How much to get screwed?"*

*"$100,"* replied the hooker.

*"$100? Are you kidding? Who do you think you are, a computer consultant?"*

**%-6 User is braindead**

# Chapter Two
# Early Internet Comedy

These are some of the general jokes from **rec.humor.funny**'s early years. A lot of the material in this book doesn't have any direct relation to the Internet or computers. However, it was all selected by computer users (nerds if you prefer) for computer users. I think that all the material here, even the general jokes (mostly sexual or political), has some special appeal to the computer using audience.

In this section, as well as in other sections, you are warned that you will see jokes with swearing and explicit sexual references. The computer network world is still a young, mostly male preserve, with a large student component and the subject matter of the humor reflects that.

Most nasty jokes here have keywords on them that tell a little about the content. These are for convenience only, and are not a guarantee that you won't be offended.

*You were warned.*

---

## WHAT GOES UP...
brunette@newton.Berkeley.EDU (Harold Lynn Brunette)
University of California, Berkeley

laugh

Oscar was an unlucky sap. Having just spent megabucks on a skydiving class, he dove out of the airplane and pulled the ripcord. The chute emerged, tangled, and he cut it free. He then pulled the cord on the reserve chute, and it was also tangled. He prayed to his God and looked down to the ground below. To his amazement, a woman was coming up with equal velocity.

*"Hey, you know anything about parachutes?"* he shouted to her as they passed by.

The reply: *"No ... you know anything about Coleman stoves?"*

---

## THE BROTHEL MAKES US STRONG
jagardner@watmath.UUCP (Jim Gardner)                              laugh, sexual

A dedicated shop steward was at a convention in Las Vegas and decided to check out the local brothels.

When he got to the first one, he asked the Madame, *"Is this a union house?"*

*"No, I'm sorry it isn't."*

*"Well, if I pay you $100, what cut do the girls get?"*

*"The house gets $80, and the girls get $20."*

Mightily offended at such unfair dealings, the man stomped off down the street in search of a more equitable shop.

His search continued as long as you want to draw things out, until finally he reached a brothel where the Madame said, *"Why yes, this is a union house."*

*"And if I pay you $100, what cut do the girls get?"*

*"The girls get $80, and the house gets $20."*

*"That's more like it!"* the man said. He looked around the room and pointed to a stunningly attractive redhead. *"I'd like her for the night."*

*"I'm sure you would, sir,"* said the Madame, gesturing to a fat fifty-year-old woman in the corner, *"but Ethel here has seniority."*

**:0 Yelling**

## CHANNEL TUNNEL
JRP1@phoenix.cambridge.ac.uk (Jonathan R. Partington)                    funny

An Englishman and a Frenchman are discussing the Channel Tunnel.

The Frenchman is saying how wonderful it is that this cooperative venture is taking place, and that he never expected the English to go to such trouble to be united to the mainland of Europe.

*"Oh that's nothing,"* says the Englishman, *"you should have seen the trouble we had digging the Channel in the first place!"*

## GRAFFITO RULES...

EWTILENI@pucc.Princeton.EDU (Eric Tilenius)
Princeton University, NJ

FREE NELSON MANDELA
(with proof of purchase)

SAVE SOVIET JEWS!
WIN VALUABLE PRIZES

SAVE THE WHALES!
Collect the entire set

## MORE SOVIET JOKES

"Henry_Cate_III.PA"@XEROX.COM
Xerox, Sunnyvale, CA

Czech walks into police station in 1968 during the Fraternal Assistance.

Czech: *Hey, out there in the street, a Swiss soldier knocked me down and took my Russian watch.*

Desk Sergeant: *Come again?*

Czech: *Are you deaf? Out there in the street, a Swiss soldier knocked me down and took my Russian watch.*

Desk Sergeant: *You're confused. It was a Russian soldier who knocked you down and took your Swiss watch.*

Czech: *Well, maybe, but you said it, not me.*

## ALIENS AMONG US

tim@attdso.att.com (Tim J Ihde)

*(And I thought it was hard to write down verbal humor . . . I'll give it a try though.)*

This was a one panel cartoon in "Aboriginal Science Fiction."

On the bridge of a flying saucer, flying over the Earth: An alien soldier and his commander.

Soldier to commander: *"Well, now that we've captured their king they'll have to surrender!"*

Behind them, bound and gagged: Elvis.

## FARM JOKE SUBMISSION

watmath!topaz.rutgers.edu!ostroff (Jack H. Ostroff)      chuckle, offense=aggies

A farmer goes into a farm supply store and orders two hundred chicks, explaining to the owner that he wants to start a chicken farm. Two weeks later, he returns to the store and buys another two hundred chicks. The owner is curious, but doesn't say anything. The same thing happens when the farmer returns in another two weeks for another two hundred chicks. When he returns for the fourth time, the owner's curiosity is too much for him, so he asks the farmer why he keeps coming back for so many chicks. The farmer says, *"Well, I guess I must be doing something wrong, but I don't know what. I think I'm either planting them too deep or too close together."*

Bemused by his lack of success, the farmer sends off a report of what he has done to the local agricultural school, asking for advice. Three weeks later, the reply comes back, saying simply, *"Please send soil sample."*

## THE HAIR O' THE DOG . . .

landry@enginr.enet.dec.com (Chris Landry DTN 227-3671)       laugh

*(True(?) story heard on WVBF, Boston:)*

Apparently this woman's miniature schnauzer had an infection in its ear. The vet told her that it was due to an ingrown hair and that the best treatment would be to remove the hair with a depilatory cream. The women went to a drug store and asked the druggist for assistance in selecting an appropriate product. He went on about how some were better for use on legs and how some were gentler and better for removing facial hair. He then said, *"May I ask where you intend to use this?"*

She replied *"Well, it's for my schnauzer."*

He said, *"OK, but you shouldn't ride a bike for two weeks."*

## ALZ LANG SYNE

heath@ncrcae.UUCP

NCR Corp., Engineering & Manufacturing - Columbia, SC      chuckle

What's the good part about Alzheimer's Disease?

*You keep meeting new friends!*

## A GENIE JOKE
"Henry_Cate_III.PA"@XEROX.COM
Xerox, Sunnyvale, CA

heard it, funny

One day an old Jewish Pole, living in Warsaw, has his last light bulb burn out. To get a new one he'll have to stand in line for two hours at the store (and they'll probably be out by the time he gets there), so he goes up to his attic and starts rummaging around for an old oil lamp he vaguely remembers seeing.

He finds the old brass lamp in the bottom of a trunk that has seen better days. He starts to polish it and (poof!) a genie appears in cloud of smoke.

*"Hoho, Mortal!"* says the genie stretching and yawning. *"For releasing me I will grant you three wishes."*

The old man thinks for a moment, and says, *"I want Genghis Khan resurrected. I want him to re-unite his Mongol hordes, march to the Polish border, and then decide he doesn't want the place and march back home."*

*"No sooner said than done!"* thunders the genie. *"Your second wish?"*

*"OK. I want Genghis Khan resurrected. I want him to re-unite his Mongol hordes, march to the Polish border, and then decide he doesn't want the place and march back home."*

*"Hmmm. Well, all right. Your third wish?"*

*"I want Genghis Khan resurrected. I want him to re-unite his —"*

*"Okokok. Right. What's this business about Genghis Khan marching to Poland and turning around again?"*

The old man smiles. *"He has to pass through Russia six times."*

**:-0 No Yelling! (Quiet Lab)**

## INTERESTING OBSERVATION
rickj@teklds.TEK.COM (Rick Jarvis)
Tektronix Inc., Beaverton, OR

laugh

...Have you ever noticed that you never see the Father, the Son, and the Holy Ghost together at the same time? Oh, sure, everybody talks like they aren't the same person, but I wonder...

## ANOTHER JOKE FROM POLAND

keithe@tekgvs.TEK.COM (Keith Ericson at TekLabs (resident factious factotum))     laugh

The line in front of the butcher shop in Warsaw is long, indeed, and the people grow weary, ever more weary, of the wait. Eventually an official comes out and announces *"We are very low on meat; all Jews must leave the line."* So the Jews in the line quit the queue and head for home, empty-handed.

After some more of a wait the same official reappears and announces, *"We are even lower on meat that we thought. All non-party members must leave the line."* So all the non-card-carrying members standing in line begin heading for home, equally empty-handed.

After some more time the official appears to declare *"All Serbs and Croats must leave the line; we haven't enough meat for you."* Disappointed, they leave the line and wander off.

Well, you guessed it: a bit later the same official appears and informs the remaining people *"Unfortunately we have run out of meat entirely — you may as well all go home,"* and disappears back into the store.

*"Isn't that just the way it always is,"* mutters one old man as he departs. *"Those damn Jews get all the breaks!"*

---

**:-( Frowning smiley**

---

## WOMAN GOES TO LAS VEGAS

warnock@hubcap.UUCP (Todd Warnock)
Clemson University, Clemson, SC

funny, sexual

A man comes home to find his wife packing her bags. *"Where are you going?"* he asked.

*"To Las Vegas! I found out that there are men that will pay me $400 to do what I do for you for free!"*

The man pondered that thought for a moment, and then began packing HIS bags. *"What do you think you are doing?"* she screamed.

*"Going to Las Vegas with you... I want to see how you live on $800 a year!"*

## A SOVIET MAN OF LETTERS

bapat@utx1.UUCP (Bapat)
the boundary between UNIX and sanity

funny

Stalin is dying, and summons Comrade Khruschev to his bedside. Wheezing his last few words with difficulty, Stalin tells Khruschev, *"Comrade, the reins of the country are now in your hands. But before I go, I want to give you some advice."*

*"Yes, yes, Great Leader, what is it,"* Khruschev asks.

Reaching under his pillow, Stalin produces two envelopes marked 1 and 2. *"Take these letters,"* he tells Khruschev. *"Keep them safely — don't open them. Only if the country is in turmoil and things start going badly, open the first one. That'll give you some advice on what to do. And, even after that, if things start going REALLY badly, open the second one."* With a gasp, Stalin breathed his last.

Well, Khruschev succeeded him, and sure enough, within a few years, things started going badly — unemployment increased, crops failed, people became restless. Nikita decided it was time to open the first letter. All it said was: *"Blame everything on me!"* So Khruschev launched a massive deStalinization campaign, and blamed Josef for all the excesses and purges and ills of the present system, and bought himself some time that way.

But things continued on the downslide — Kennedy successfully rebuffed Soviet missiles in Cuba, unemployment increased even more, crops failed even more, the Politburo was unhappy with Khruschev's leadership and upstarts like Brezhnev and Gromyko were threatening his credibility. So finally, after much deliberation, Nikita opened the second letter.

All it said was: *"Write two letters."*

## I OWE, I OWE

davef@brspyr1.BRS.Com (Dave Fiske)
BRS Info Technologies, Latham NY

chuckle

Wife: *Okay, today's Friday. Where's your pay envelope?*

Man: *I already spent all my pay. I bought something for the house.*

Wife: *What? What could you buy for the house that cost $480?*

Man: *Eight rounds of drinks.*

>;-> Winky and devil combined smiley

## REVENGE

coscklq@uhnix1.UUCP (5412)

University of Houston                                                    gross, funny

A construction worker came home just in time to find his wife in bed with another man. (*Sounds familiar, right?*) So he dragged the man down the stairs to the garage and puts his John Thomas in a vise. He secured it tightly and removed the handle. Then he picked up a hacksaw.

The man, terrified, screamed, *"STOP! STOP! YOU'RE NOT GOING TO.. TO.. CUT IT OFF, ARE YOU???!?"*

The husband said, with a gleam of revenge in his eye:

*"Nope. You are. I'm going to set the garage on fire."*

:-I Indifferent smiley

## WORLD WAR II JOKE

ao@cevax.berkeley.edu (A. Ozselcuk)

University of California, Berkeley                             laugh, heard it, swearing

A World War II pilot is reminiscing before school children about his days in the air force. (*Joke best delivered with a good thick accent.*)

*"In 1942,"* he says, *"the situation was really tough. The Germans had a very strong air force. I remember,"* he continues, *"one day I was protecting the bombers and suddenly, out of the clouds, these fokkers appeared.*

(At this point, several of the children giggle.)

*I looked up, and right above me was one of them. I aimed at him and shot him down. They were swarming. I immediately realized that there was another fokker behind me."*

At this instant the girls in the auditorium start to giggle and boys start to laugh. The teacher stands up and says, *"I think I should point out that 'Fokker' was the name of the German-Dutch aircraft company"*

*"That's true,"* says the pilot, *"but these fokkers were flying Messerschmidts."*

## A NICE PUT-DOWN

bzs@bu-cs.BU.EDU (Barry Shein)
Boston U. Comp. Sci.

funny

Do you mind if I smoke?

*I don't care if you burst into flames and die.*

## CHURCH BULLETIN HUMOR

brent@questar.QUESTAR.MN.ORG (Nordquist)
Questar Data Systems, Minneapolis

laugh

(DISCLAIMER: I am a Christian; my point is thus obviously not to blast the Church. I just found these very amusing.)

### SENTENCES WHICH ACTUALLY APPEARED IN A CHURCH BULLETIN OR WERE ANNOUNCED IN A SERVICE

This afternoon there will be a meeting in the South and North ends of the church. Children will be baptized at both ends.

Tuesday at 4 P.M. there will be an ice cream social. Will ladies giving milk, please come early.

Wednesday, the Ladies Literary Society will meet. Mrs. Johns will sing "Put Me In My Little Bed" accompanied by the Pastor.

Thursday at 5 P.M. there will be a meeting of the Little Mothers Club. All wishing to become Little Mothers will please meet the Minister in his study.

This being Easter Sunday, we will ask Mrs. Jackson to come forward and lay an egg on the altar.

The service will close with "Little Drops of Water." One of the ladies will start quietly and the rest of the congregation will join her.

On Sunday, a special collection will be taken to defray the expenses of the new carpeting. All wishing to do something on the carpet, please come forward and get a piece of paper.

The ladies of the Church have cast off clothing of every kind. They may be seen in the basement on Friday afternoon.

This evening at 7 P.M. there will be a hymn sing in the park across from the Church. Bring a blanket and come prepared to sin.

## CHEAP AT HALF THE PRICE

UH2@psuvm.bitnet (Lee Sailer)

laugh, sexual

*Chet Wolford tells this one:*

An Erie, Pennsylvania executive with a new young wife and a yen for golf decided about December one year that he couldn't take it any longer. So he said to his wife one evening, *"Honey, next Friday we're going to Hilton Head for the weekend. We'll get a condo on the golf course and I'm going to play golf all weekend."*

*"That sounds fine,"* she purred. And, sure enough, next Saturday morning at 6 a.m., found him on the golf course, all alone. After playing two holes, he noticed a man carrying a golf bag walking toward him across a fairway. The exec. waited, and the other man arrived, saying, *"Mind if I play along?"*

The exec. said, *"Fine. Glad to have the company."*

All went well for a couple of holes, until each approached the sixth green. When the new fellow laid down his clubs, the cover came off one club. The exec. noticed, however, that it wasn't a club at all. It was a high powered rifle.

*"Whoa,"* he said. *"That's a high powered rifle!"*

*"Look,"* said the other man. *"I'm not out to cause any trouble. If you want me to leave, I will. No hard feelings."*

*"No. No,"* said the exec. *"I'm just curious as to why you have a high-powered rifle in your bag."*

The other man pondered for a moment and then said, *"Well, I'll tell you. It's my business. It's what I do for a living."*

*"Wow,"* said the other. *"I've heard about guys like you, but I've never met one before."*

*"Still want me to play?"* said the other.

*"Sure,"* said the Erie exec. *"As a matter of fact, you know, I do a little hunting. Would you mind if I look at it?"*

The other man showed him the rifle. It was beautiful—an inlaid Weatherby with a huge powerful scope mounted on it.

The exec. picked it up, looked through the scope, and said, *"Gee, I can see the window of my condo with this thing. Matter of fact, there's my wife."* He lowered the gun for a moment and said, *"she doesn't have any clothes on."* He looked through the scope again. *"Damn, there's a guy with her."*

The Erie exec. lowered the rifle and looked at the other man. *"How much do you charge?"*

*"$10,000 a bullet,"* said the man.

The Erie man thought for a moment, and said, *"Do it."*

*"Which one?"* said the hit man.

*"Both,"* said the exec.

*"That's $20,000, you know."*

*"I don't care. Hit 'em both."*

The hit man took two cartridges from his bag and loaded the rifle. *"Where do you want me to get the man?"* he asked.

*"You know where to hit him,"* said the exec.

*"How about the woman?"*

*"In the mouth. She's always flapping her gums anyway."*

*"OK,"* said the hit man as he raised the rifle. Taking careful aim, he clicked off the safety, but then he paused and chuckled. *"Mister,"* he said, *"I think I'm going to be able to save you ten thousand dollars."*

---

**:-> Sarcastic smilie**

---

## GREEK HORSES?

richard@gryphon.CTS.COM (Richard Sexton)                    funny, heard it

Middle of the night, middle of nowhere, two cars both slightly cross over the white line in the center of the road. They collide and a fair amount of damage is done, although neither driver is hurt. It's impossible to assess blame for the accident on either, however.

They both get out. One is a doctor, one is a lawyer. The lawyer calls the police on his car phone; they'll be there in 20 minutes.

It's cold and damp, and both men are shaken up. The lawyer offers the doctor a drink of brandy from his hip flask, the doctor accepts, drinks and hands it back to the lawyer, who puts it away.

*"Aren't you going to have a drink?"* the doctor says.

*"AFTER the police get here,"* replies the lawyer.

## COMRADE STALIN

janw@inmet.UUCP

chuckle

Lenin is dying, and talking things over with Stalin, his successor.

*"The one worry I have,"* says Lenin, *"is this: will the people follow you? What do you think, comrade Stalin?"*

*"They will,"* says Stalin, *"they surely will."*

*"I hope so,"* says Lenin, *"but what if they don't follow you?"*

*"No problem,"* says Stalin, *"then they'll follow you."*

## THE ROYAL OUTING

rlw@philabs.philips.com

laugh, sexual, offense=loyalists

Her Majesty, the Queen, and Her Royal Highness, Princess Diana, were out for a drive in the country. Suddenly, upon a quiet road, they were set upon and stopped by a highwayman. He forced them out of the car at gunpoint, and demanded their jewels.

*"Give me your tiara, Ma'am,"* demanded the robber.

*"I'm sorry,"* replied the Queen. *"I did not wear my tiara today."*

*"Well then, give me your ring, your highness!"* demanded the robber.

*"I'm sorry, but I didn't wear my ring today,"* replied the Princess.

Frustrated, the robber waved them away, and drove off with the Bentley, getting at least something for his efforts. The Queen, Princess and their chauffeur made it back to Windsor castle, where they related their ordeal to the Queen Mother.

After the Queen Mother received an account of the robbery she turned to Queen Elizabeth and asked, "I thought that you wore your tiara today?"

*"But I did. When I saw the robber pull us over, I hid the tiara in my private place."*

The Queen Mother turned towards Diana and said, *"And you — I thought you wore your ring today?"*

*"I did, but like Momsie, I hid the ring in my private place."*

At this point the chauffeur interjected, *"It's a shame, Ma'am, that Princess Margaret wasn't wi' us. We could have saved the Bentley!"*

## NEWFIE FLIES TO TORONTO

rapin@bnrmtv.UUCP (Eric Rapin)
Bell Northern Research, Mtn. View, CA

funny, offense=newfies

[Ed: Original from: Reg.Cable.7M45@bnrcgl]

A Newfie was going to Toronto on the Airplane and started talking to a Mainlander.

Newfie: *Lord Tundrin' Geese's Bye, What do you do for a livin?*

Mainlander: *Well, I'm a Psychoanalyst.*

Newfie: *Psychoanalyst, What the Heck is that?*

Mainlander: *It's hard to explain so I'll give you an example.*

Mainlander: *Do you own a Fishtank?*

Newfie: Yes, I got a tank.

Mainlander: *Well, I bet you like fish then?*

Newfie: *Yeah, I like fish.*

Mainlander: *Well, if you like fish then you probably like the water.*

Newfie: *Yeah, I love the water.*

Mainlander: *Well, if you like the water, then you probably like to go to the beach.*

Newfie: *I love to go the beach.*

Mainlander: *I bet you like to look at girls in bikinis while you're at the beach.*

Newfie: *You betcha.*

Mainlander: *And as you're looking at girls on the beach I bet you think about taking them home and having your way with them.*

Newfie: *Gosh, How did you know that?*

Mainlander: *Well, that's what a Psychoanalyst is.*

Newfie: *Oh.*

The Newfie was going back to St. John's and started to talk to another Mainlander on the plane.

Newfie: *Hi, How ya doin?*

Mainlander: *Oh, fine I guess.*

Newfie: *I'm a Psychoanalyst.*

Mainlander: *You're a Psychoanalyst?*

Newfie: *Yeah, let me explain it to ya.*

Newfie: *Do you own a fishtank?*

Mainlander: *No.*

Newfie: *What are ya!? Some kind of faggot?*

---

**(-: User is left-handed**

---

## THE CHEMISTRY SET

cm2n+@andrew.cmu.edu (Christopher A. Maloney)
Carnegie Mellon University

chuckle, sexual

*Here's one I heard on the radio.*

A father comes home and asks where his son is. His wife replies that he's downstairs playing with his new chemistry set. The father is curious so he wanders down stairs to see what his son is doing. As he's walking down the steps he hears a banging sound. When he gets to the bottom he sees his son pounding a nail into the wall. He says to his son, *"What are you doing? I thought you were playing with your chemistry set. Why are you hammering a nail into the wall?"* His son replied, *"This isn't a nail, dad, it's a worm. I put these chemicals on it and it became hard as a rock."*

His dad thought about it for a minute and said, *"I'll tell you what son, give me those chemicals and I'll give you a new Volkswagen."* His son quite naturally said, *"Sure why not."*

The next day his son went into the garage to see his new car. Parked in the garage was a brand new Mercedes. Just then his dad walked in. He asked his father where his Volkswagen was. His dad replied, *"It's right there behind the Mercedes. By the way, the Mercedes is from your mother."*

---

**K:P Little kid with a propeller beanie**

---

## A *REAL* HONEST-TO-GOODNESS MORMON JOKE

mroz@hudson.steinmetz (Mroz)
General Electric CRD, Schenectady, NY                                          chuckle, sexual

*(What with all the talk about Mormon jokes here's a REAL MORMON JOKE! At last!)*

A woman visiting Salt Lake City in the latter half of the 19th century sees someone that she thinks may be Brigham Young, the leader of the Mormon church.

Woman: *"Are you Brigham Young?"*

Brigham Young: *"I am."*

Woman: *"Are you the Brigham Young that is the head of the Mormon church?"*

Brigham Young: *"I am."*

Woman: *"Are you the Brigham Young that led the Mormons to Utah?"*

Brigham Young: *"I am."*

Woman: *"Are you the Brigham Young that denounces all Christian religions as false except Mormonism?"*

Brigham Young: *"I am."*

About this time, the woman is beginning to lose her temper.

Woman: *"Are you the Brigham Young who preaches polygamy?"*

Brigham Young: *"I am."*

Now she's really getting mad.

Woman: *"Are you the Brigham Young who has 26 wives?"*

Brigham Young: *"I am."*

Then furiously, she says —

Woman: *"You ought to be Hung!"*

Brigham Young: *"I am."*

## ENDORSED BY THE ALMIGHTY

gc1a+@andrew.cmu.edu (Glenn Cassidy)                                          chuckle

*The following is a promotional spot heard on a college radio station:*
*"Hello, this is God. Whenever I'm in Pittsburgh—which is all the time, since I'm omnipresent—I listen to all the radio stations at once, including WRCT."*

## POLISH BANK JOKE

davef@brspyr1.BRS.Com (Dave Fiske)
BRS Info Technologies, Latham NY

laugh

*Back during the Solidarity days, I heard that the following joke was being told in Poland:*

A man goes into the Bank of Gdansk to make a deposit. Since he has never kept money in a bank before, he is a little nervous.

*"What happens if the Bank of Gdansk should fail?"* he asks.

*"Well, in that case your money would be insured by the Bank of Warsaw."*

*"But, what if the Bank of Warsaw fails?"*

*"Well, there'd be no problem, because the Bank of Warsaw is insured by the National Bank of Poland."*

*"And if the National Bank of Poland fails?"*

*"Then your money would be insured by the Bank of Moscow."*

*"And what if the Bank of Moscow fails?"*

*"Then your money would be insured by the Great Bank of the Soviet Union."*

*"And if that bank fails?"*

*"Well, in that case, you'd lose all your money. But, wouldn't it be worth it?"*

**:*) Drunk smiley**

## RUSSIAN JOKE (yet another)

goldberg@russell.stanford.edu (Jeffrey Goldberg)
Center for the Study of Language and Information, Stanford U.

chuckle

An old woman was sitting in a park in Moscow reading a "Teach Yourself Hebrew" book. A policeman notices her and decides to start to give her a hard time.

*"What are you reading that for?"* he shouts at her.

She replies, *"I am old, and I will die soon. I want to be prepared, so I am studying the language of heaven."*

The cop says, *"Well, how do know that it's heaven that you are going to?"*

The old women answers, *"Well, honestly I don't, but that's okay. I already speak Russian."*

## WHAT YOU SHOULDN'T SAY TO YOUR WIFE...

dsg@mitre-bedford.ARPA (David S. Goldberg)
The MITRE Corporation, Bedford, Mass.

chuckle, sexual

*This isn't mine, I heard it on the radio.*

Man's wife asks him to go to the store to buy some cigarettes. So he walks down to the store only to find it closed. So he goes into a nearby bar to use the vending machine. At the bar he sees a beautiful woman and starts talking to her. They have a couple of beers and one thing leads to another and they end up in her apartment. After they've had their fun, he realizes it's 3 AM and says, *"Oh no, it's so late, my wife's going to kill me. Have you got any talcum powder?"* She gives him some talcum powder, which he proceeds to rub on his hands and then he goes home.

His wife is waiting for him in the doorway and she is pretty pissed. *"Where the hell have you been?!?!"*

*"Well, honey, it's like this. I went to the store like you asked, but they were closed. So I went to the bar to use the vending machine. I saw this great looking chick there and we had a few drinks and one thing led to another and I ended up in bed with her."*

*"Oh yeah? Let me see your hands!"*

She sees his hands are covered with powder and ... *"You God damn liar!!! You went bowling again!!!"*

## ICEFISHING

crick@bnr-rsc.UUCP (Bill Crick)
Bell-Northern Research, Ottawa, Canada

offense=newfies, chuckle

This Newfie is going icefishing. He starts to drill a hole with his auger when a loud booming voice says, *"THERE'S NO FISH DOWN THERE!"*

So he stops drilling and moves a little ways and starts to drill again. The same voice booms, *"THERE'S NO FISH DOWN THERE!"*

So he moves a little further and is about to drill again, but the voice immediately comes again, *"THERE'S NO FISH THERE EITHER!"*

The Newf looks around and says, *"Who are you anyways? God?"*

*"NO I'M THE ARENA MANAGER!"*

## PURCHASING, YOU KNOW...

chris@spock (Chris Ott)
Computer-Aided Engineering Lab (CAEL), University of Arizona

funny, sexual

A man goes into a drug store and asks the cashier for some rubbers. The cashier asks, *"What size?"*

The man replies, *"Size? I didn't know they came in sizes."*

*"Yes, they do,"* she says, *"What size do you want?"*

*"Well, gee, I don't know,"* the man answers.

The lady is used to this, so she tells him to go to the back yard and measure his dick by sticking it into each of the three holes in the fence. While the man is back there, the lady sneaks around to the other side of the fence and spreads her legs behind each hole as the man tests it. When they return, the cashier asks, *"What will it be? Small, medium, or large?"*

The man replies, *"To hell with the rubbers, give me a hundred feet of that fence back there!"*

**[:] User is a robot**

## AGE OLD JOKE?

scott@ubvax.UUCP (Scott Scheiman)

funny

A lady is having a bad day at the roulette tables in 'Vegas. She's down to her last $50. Exasperated, she exclaims, *"What rotten luck! What in the world should I do now?"* A man standing next to her, trying to calm her down suggests, *"I don't know ... why don't you play your age?"*

He walks away. Moments later, his attention is grabbed by a great commotion at the roulette table. Maybe she won! He rushes back to the table and pushes his way through the crowd. The lady is laying limp on the floor, with the table operator kneeling over her.

The man is stunned. He asks, *"What happened? Is she all right?"* The operator replies, *"I don't know. She put all her money on 29 and 36 came up. Then she just fainted!"*

## CAPITALIST HELL VS COMMUNIST HELL

"Henry_Cate_III.PA"@XEROX.COM
Xerox, Sunnyvale, CA

funny

A political activist named Dave was just arriving in Hell, and was told he had a choice to make. He could go to Capitalist Hell or to Communist Hell.

Naturally, Dave wanted to compare the two, so he wandered over to Capitalist Hell. There outside the door was Rockefeller, *looking bored.* "*What's it like in there?*" asked Dave. "*Well,*" he replied, "*In Capitalist Hell, they flay you alive, boil you in oil, chain you to a rock and let a vulture tear your liver out, and cut you up into small pieces with sharp knives.*"

"*That's terrible!!*" gasped Dave. "*I'm going to check out Communist Hell!*" He went over to Communist Hell, where he discovered a huge line of people waiting to get in; the line circled around the lobby seven times before receding off into the horizon. Dave pushed his way through to the head of the line, where he found Karl Marx busily signing people in. Dave asked Karl what Communist Hell was like.

"*In Communist Hell,*" said Marx impatiently, "*they flay you alive, boil you in oil, chain you to a rock and let vultures tear out your liver, and cut you up into small pieces with sharp knives.*"

"*But ... but that's the same as Capitalist Hell!*" protested Dave.

"*True,*" sighed Marx, "*but sometimes we don't have oil, sometimes we don't have knives ...*"

## BAD DANDRUFF PUN

andrew@teletron.UUCP (Andrew Scott)

sexual

A young girl was at the doctor's for a checkup:

"*By the way, Doctor, my boyfriend has dandruff. Is there anything you might suggest?*"

"*Why don't you just give him Head & Shoulders?*"

After a short pause,

"*How do you give shoulders?*"

`8-) User is wearing sunglasses`

## BALLS TO YOUR PARTNER

shankar@hpclscu.HP.COM (Shankar Unni)
HP NSG/ISD Computer Language Lab

chuckle

An American General, a Russian General and a British General are standing on the deck of a ship watching war exercises. *(OK, OK, so this is an old one.)* The topic of discussion turns to human courage, and the Russian General boasts, *"Russians are the most courageous people on Earth!"*

Upon which the American (naturally) challenges him: *"Oh YEAH?"*

The Russian says, *"Sure! Here, Yuri! Jump off the deck (into the freezing Atlantic) and swim around the ship!"*

Yuri marches off without a word, and does as he is told. The Russian turns around and says: *"See, there's an example of courage!"*

The American has to top this, so he calls up one of his underlings and gives him the order:

*"Jack, Jump off the main mast into the ocean, and swim around the ship seven times!"*

Poor Jack goes off without a murmur, and he too does as he is told. The American General says: *"Now top that for courage!"*

So they both turn around to the British General who has been standing around watching these antics silently. They ask him: *"What about your people?"*

So the British guy calls up one of his people and says: *"Trevor, jump off the mast and swim under the keel of the ship, will you, old chap?"*

Trevor stares at his general.

*"Let me get this right. You want me to jump off the mast."*

*"Yes."*

*"And swim under the keel"*

*"Yes."*

*"You must be daft!"*

And so saying, Trevor turns around and saunters off. Whereupon the British General turns to the other two and says,

*"Now there's an example of TRUE courage!"*

---

B:-) Sunglasses on head

---

## USEFUL PHRASES TO KNOW WHEN TRAVELING IN MOSLEM AREAS
doug@wiley.UUCP

*racist, chuckle*

*This is from a multi-generation Xerox copy that was given to me by someone I know. I have no idea where it came it from or if it is accurate, but it is amusing nonetheless.*

AKBAR KHALI-KILI HAFTIR LOTFAN.
Thank you for showing me your marvelous gun.

FEKR GABUL CRADAN DAVAT PAEH GUSH DIVAR.
I am delighted to accept your kind invitation to lie on the floor
with my arms above my head and my legs apart.

SHOMAEH FEKR TAMOMEH OEH GOFTEH BANDE.
I agree with everything you have ever said or thought in your life.

AUTO ARREREGH DAVATEMAN MANO SEPAHEH HAST.
It is exceptionally kind of you to allow me to
travel in the trunk of your car.

FASHAL-EH TUPEHMAN NA DEGAT MANO GOFTAM
CHEESHAYEH MOHEMARA JEBEHKESHVAREHMAN.
If you will do me the kindness of not harming my genital appendages
I will gladly reciprocate by betraying my country in public.

KHREL JEPAHEH MANEH VA JAYEH AMERIKAHEY.
I will tell you the names and addresses
of many American spies traveling as reporters.

BALLI, BALLI, BALLI !
Whatever you say!

MATERNIER GHERMEZ AHLEIEH, GHORBAN.
The red blindfold will be lovely, excellency.

TIEKH NUNEH OB KHRELEH BEZORG
VA KHRUBE BOYAST INO BEGERAM.
The water-soaked bread crumbs are delicious,
thank you. I must have the recipe.

[Ed: Reportedly these phrases are actually garbled Persian!]

## WHAT HURTS THE MOST

okrieg@godzilla.ele.toronto.edu (Orran Y. Krieger)

sexual, chuckle

A group of guys and one girl are sitting together at a ball game. During the game the guys notice that the girl knows just as much about the game as themselves, and are really impressed.

After the game they ask her *"how is it that you know so much about baseball?"*

She says, *"Well, I used to be a guy and got a sex change."*

The guys are amazed, but very curious about the process. *"what was the most painful part of the process? Was it when they cut off your penis?"*

*"That was very painful, but was not the most painful part."*

*"Was it when they cut off your balls?"*

*"That was very painful, but was not the most painful part."*

*"What was the most painful part?"*

*"The part that hurt the most was when they cut my salary in half!"*

[Ed: I thought this was a nice variant of this usually anti-female joke, although I think the other one ("when they scooped out half my brains") is funnier for its sheer offensiveness.]

**8:-) User is a little girl**

## FISH STORY

johnbl@tekig5.TEK.COM (John Blankenagel)
Tektronix Inc., Beaverton, OR

chuckle

A lawyer and an engineer <or some other honest profession member :-) > were fishing in the Caribbean. The lawyer said, *"I am here because my house burned down and everything I owned was burned. The insurance company paid for everything."*

*"That is quite a coincidence,"* said the engineer, *"I am here because my house and all my belongings were destroyed by a flood, and my insurance company also paid for everything."*

The lawyer looked somewhat confused and asked, *"how do you start a flood?"*

## MORE IN THE COURT
rburgess@leadsv.UUCP (Rebecca Burgess)                                    chuckle

*Heard on one of those starving artist/comedian TV shows:*

Just once, I would like to see an intelligent witness on the stand:

Prosecutor: *Did you kill the victim?*

Defendant: *No, I did not.*

P: *Do you know what the penalties are for perjury?*

D: *Yes, I do. And they're a hell of a lot better than the penalty for murder.*

## IMMUNITY?
gazit%ganelon.usc.edu@oberon.USC.EDU (Salit)              funny, offense=Romanians

The American ambassador visited the Romanian president. In the waiting room he talked with two of the ministers for five minutes.

When he entered he said to the Romanian president, *"I really don't want to bother you but I talked with two of your ministers, and my gold watch was disappeared."*

So the president answered, *"OK. I'll take care of it,"* left the room and came back two minutes later with the watch.

The ambassador said, *"Thank you very much,"* said the ambassador. *"I hope that I didn't cause any crisis between you and them."*

*"That's OK,"* said the president. *"They did not notice."*

## TELL IT TO THE MARINES
edw@pinot (Ed Wright)
Zehn and The Art of ATE.                                  sexual, offense=USMC, funny

A little kid watched the drunk marine go into the bathroom. As the marine was taking a leak the kid asked, *"Are you really a marine?"* The marine replied, *"Yes, do you want to wear my hat?"* The kid said, *"Oh yes,"* and the marine gave him his hat.

A minute later a sailor walked into the restroom and the kid said, *"Are you really a sailor?"* The sailor said, *"Yeah ... ya wanta suck my cock?"* The kid pulled off his hat and said, *"Oh no!! I'm not really a marine!"*

## YOU ALMOST GOT ME KILT!

w25y@vax5.CCS.CORNELL.EDU
Cornell Computer Service, Ithaca NY

sexual, funny

A Scotsman clad in a kilt walks up to the counter in an Apothecary. From his pocket he takes a heavily used plaid condom that is torn, patched, sewn and is currently split down one side. He asks the proprietor, *"How much to replace this, Ian?"* The proprietor says, *"Why, Angus, that'll be four pence."* Then the Scotsman asks, *"How much to repair?"* The proprietor looks the condom over carefully and says, *"Three pence to repair."* The Scotsman ponders for a moment, then says, *"I'll be back."*

Later in the day, the Scotsman returns with a smile on his face and says, *"Ian, the Regiment has voted to repair!"*

— Bilbo Baggins

## LUCK OF THE IRISH

leonard%iros1.UUCP (Nicolas Leonard)

funny

Two Irish lovers are sitting on a bench, in a park. They are holding hands, but the lady is nervously twisting her hands.

Mary: *"Patrick. I have something to tell you."*

Patrick: *"Well, what's on your mind? You know you can tell me everything."*

Mary: *"It's so terrible."*

Patrick: *"You know you can trust me. What is it?"*

Mary: *"Well, it was a few years ago. Father lost his job, and no money in sight.."*

Patrick: *"So, what is it?"*

Mary: *"Oh. We were so desperate. For some time I had to turn ... prostitute!"*

Patrick: *"WHAT!"*

Mary: *"We needed the money so bad!"*

Patrick: *"There is no good reason for this! Endangering your very soul! How could you? YOU! Mary, this is more than I can stand!"*

Mary: *"Not you, Pat! No! I thought you'd understand. I thought you could still love me, even though I had been a whore."*

Patrick: *"Oh! ...You... Well, that's OK. For a moment I thought you said 'Protestant'!"*

## GETTING STONED

djsalomon@watdragon.UUCP (Daniel J. Salomon)                                    sacrilege

Jesus came across an adulteress crouching in a corner with a crowd around her preparing to stone her to death. Jesus stopped them and said, *"Let he who is without sin cast the first stone."* Suddenly a woman at the back of the crowd fired off a stone at the adulteress. At which point Jesus looked over and said, *"Mother! Sometimes you really TICK ME OFF."*

## FURRIER AND FURRIER

brunette@newton.Berkeley.EDU (Harold Lynn Brunette)
University of California, Berkeley                                              funny

*(Here's one I wish I'd written:)*

A man and a woman walk into a very posh Rodeo Drive furrier. *"Show the lady your finest mink!"* the fellow exclaims. So the owner of the shop goes in back and comes out with an absolutely gorgeous full-length coat. As the lady tries it on, the furrier sidles up to the guy and discreetly whispers, *"Ah, sir, that particular fur goes for $65,000."*

*"No problem! I'll write you a check!"*

*"Very good, sir."* says the shop owner. *"Today is Saturday. You may come by on Monday to pick it up, after the check has cleared."*

So the man and the woman leave. On Monday, the fellow returns. The store owner is outraged: *"How dare you show your face in here?! There wasn't a single penny in your checking account!!"*

*"I just had to come by,"* grinned the guy, *"to thank you for the most wonderful weekend of my life!"*

## MANNERS

robert@setting.weitek.UUCP (Robert Plamondon)
WEITEK Corporation, Sunnyvale CA                                chuckle, offense=Christians

On the third day, Jesus rose, shoved open the door of his tomb, and walked again on earth.

As he was leaving, a passer-by pointed at the door Jesus had left open.

*"What's the matter with you?"* he said. *"Born in a barn?"*

## I SEE THINGS DIFFERENTLY . . .

kilroy@brillig.umd.edu (Darren F. Provine)

laugh, sexual

*(This is a joke told by the Greaseman, a DJ on DC-101, a Washington radio station:)*

Once upon a time, there was a woman working at a lingerie counter, and a customer came to the counter with a pair of frilly panties and said she'd like to buy them adding, *"but only if you can embroider 'If you can read this, you're too close' on the back."*

So, the saleswoman took the panties to the tailor in back, and described the rather unusual request.

The tailor said, *"Well, she sounds like a stick in the mud, but I can do that. Does she want block letters or script?"*

Since the saleswoman didn't know, she went back around to the counter, and asked, *"do you want that in block letters or script?"*

The customer replied, with a smile, *"Braille."*

**:-)-8 User is a Big girl**

## REAL LIFE HUMOR

langbein@topaz.rutgers.edu (John E. Langbein)
Rutgers Univ., New Brunswick, NJ

Harry was in the hospital. He was an old man. Anyway there was this young nurse. Everytime she came in, she talked to him like a little child. She would say in a patronizing tone of voice *"And how are we doing this morning??!!!"*

Well, this is a story of revenge. He had received breakfast, and pulled the juice off the tray, and put it on his stand. He had been given a Urine Bottle to fill. The juice was apple juice. You know where the juice went.

The nurse came in and picked up the urine bottle. She looks at it. *"It seems we are a little cloudy today..."* At this, he snatches the bottle out of her hand, pops off the top, and chugs it, saying

*"Well, I'll run it through again, and maybe I can filter it better this time."*

## VASELINE SALESMAN

grant@looking.UUCP (Grant Robinson)                                    sexual, chuckle

A Vaseline salesman is driving through the country, when his car starts leaking and loses all its oil. Not knowing what to do, he fills the engine with Vaseline, thinking that it is similar to oil, and drives away. It works fine until about half an hour later, when the engine gets real warm, and the Vaseline melts, and runs out through the same hole as the oil did. This time there is a farm nearby, so he decides to look for a phone.

Meanwhile, inside the farmhouse, the farmer, his wife, and daughter are having a fight about who's going to do the dishes. *"I did them this morning,"* complains the farmer. *"Well I did them at lunch,"* says his wife. *"And I'm tired from doing all the farmwork,"* says the daughter. So the farmer, in a stroke of brilliance, decides that they will settle it by all taking off their clothes, lying on the floor, and declaring that the first one to speak gets to do the dishes.

The Vaseline salesman gets to the front door, and rings the bell. No one answers so he goes in and looks for a phone. He eventually stumbles into the kitchen, and ignoring the odd sight, asks for a phone. No one answers, so he goes and looks some more. Still no luck, so he goes back to the kitchen. They still won't answer, so he decides to see what else he can get away with. He has sex with the daughter several times, bemused by her silence, then finally goes and looks for the phone again. A while later, he comes back, looks at the wife, and says, *"Why not?"* After having sex with the farmer's wife, he is getting tired and exasperated. He thinks, maybe if they have some Vaseline, I can drive my car for another half-hour. So he asks, *"Do you have any Vaseline?"* at which the farmer jumps up and yells, *"I'll do the dishes!"*

## BUYING ASPIRIN

ken@rochester.UUCP (Ken Yap)                                                    chuckle

Joe has always had an uncontrollable twitch in his left eyelid since young. Fred has a splitting headache and asks Joe to go get some aspirins. Half an hour later Joe comes back with a dozen packets of condoms.

*"I asked you to get me aspirins, not condoms."*

*"Yeah, I went to a dozen drug stores, but have you ever tried asking for aspirin with a tic in your eye?"*

## UP HIGH
hb@pixar.UUCP (H. B. Siegel)
Pixar— Marin County, California

swearing

Two guys are drinking in the bar on the 110th floor of the World Trade Center. They've both been drinking heavily for several hours and are really toasted.

The first guy slurs, *"Didja know that 'cause of the way these two buildings are set up, I could jump outa this window an' fall 'bout hunnerd floors, and the updraft between these two towers would sweep me up back into this bar?"*

The second guy doesn't believe this at all and offers to bet one hundred dollars that it wouldn't work.

The first guy says, *"You're on,"* and they each lay a crisp new hundred dollar bill on the table. He then staggers up to the window, opens it and jumps.

The second guy leans out the window to watch him fall...

10-20-30-50-80-100 stories he falls, when suddenly he gets swept back up into the bar.

The second guy is amazed and says, *"Lemme try that,"* and proceeds to jump out the window.

The first guy leans out the window to watch him fall...

10-20-30-50-80-100-110 SPLAT!— where he falls to his death.

The first guy smirks a little, grabs the two hundred dollars and walks out of the bar.

As he's walking out, the bartender says, *"You know, when you're drunk, you can be a real prick, Superman."*

**::-) User wears normal glasses**

## CHRISTMAS GIFT?
brucec@astroatc.UUCP (Bruce Cantrall)
Astronautics Technology Cntr, Madison, WI

sexual, chuckle

Q: What do you give to a man who has everything?

*A: Condoms!*

## BANGETY BANG BANG
wanttaja@ssc-vax.UUCP (Ronald J Wanttaja)

Seems there was a young soldier, who, just before battle, told his sergeant that he didn't have a rifle.

*"That's no problem, son,"* said the sergeant. *"Here, take this broom. Just point it at the Germans, and go 'Bangety Bang Bang'."*

*"But what about a bayonet, Sarge?"* asked the young (and gullible) recruit.

The sergeant pulls a piece of straw from the end of the broom, and attaches it to the handle end. *"Here, use this... just go, 'Stabity Stab Stab'."*

The recruit ends up alone on the battlefield, holding just his broom. Suddenly, a German soldier charges at him.

The recruit points the broom. "Bangety Bang Bang!" The German falls dead. More Germans appear. The recruit, amazed at his good luck, goes *"Bangety Bang Bang! Stabity Stab Stab!"* He mows down the enemy by the dozens.

Finally, the battlefield is clear, except for one German soldier walking slowly toward him. *"Bangety Bang Bang!"* shouts the recruit.

The German keeps coming.

*"Bangety Bang Bang!"* repeats the recruit, to no avail. He gets desperate. *"Bangety Bang Bang! Stabity Stab Stab!"*

It's no use. The German keeps coming. He stomps the recruit into the ground, and says...

*"Tankety Tank Tank."*

---

**B-) User wears horn-rimmed glasses**

---

## LET'S PICK ON THE ECONOMISTS
coltoff@prc.unisys.com (Joel Coltoff)     chuckle

An economist is back in his old college town many years after graduation and decides to drop in on one of his old professors. He happens to see a copy of an exam sitting on the desk, so he picks it up to look at it. Upon deciding that it looks familiar, he comments to the professor that it is the same exam that he had taken 10 years ago. The professor assures him that this is correct, but adds that this time the answers are different.

## GOD BLESS THEM ALL

inmet!bob (Bob Jordan Esq.)                                    sexual, funny

A man decided that it was time to teach his son how to say prayers, so he spent a few nights teaching the son the basics. After the kid had learned them well enough to say on his own, the father instructed him that after he was done with the prayers each night, he was to choose someone special and ask for God's blessing for that person.

Well, little kids don't always realize that their pets aren't a person, so the first night the little boy said his prayers, he ended with *"And God, please bless my puppy."* The guy thought that it was pretty cute. However, the next morning the little dog ran out the door and was killed by a car.

That night the little kid asked God to bless his cat when the prayers were finished. And, sure enough, the next morning the cat slipped out and took on the biggest dog in the neighborhood and became breakfast. The father had started to make a connection here, but decided that it was just coincidence.

But when the kid asked God to bless his goldfish, the father couldn't wait for morning so that he could check up on it. As soon as he looked in the bowl, he saw the fish floating upside down on the top.

That night the little kid ended with *"God, please give an extra special blessing to my father."*

The father couldn't sleep. He couldn't eat breakfast in the morning. He was afraid to drive to work. He couldn't get any work done because he was petrified. Finally quitting time came and he walked home, expecting to drop dead any minute.

When he arrived home, the house was a mess. His wife was lying on the couch still dressed in her robe. The dishes from breakfast were still on the table and the father was furious. He started yelling at his wife, telling her that he had had the worst day of his life and she hadn't even gotten dressed. She looked at him and said, *"Shut up! My day was worse. The mailman had a heart attack on our front porch!"*

## OVERHEARD FROM A SOVIET DIPLOMAT

lewis@rocky.STANFORD.EDU (Bil Lewis)
Stanford University Computer Science Department

heard it, funny

(Yes, this is NOT my own. I heard it at a party in Sweden, being told by a low member of the Soviet corps. there.)

So Gorbachev decided that now that he was on top, it was time to impress his ancient mother. He sent his private helicopter out to the small town where she lived to pick her up. He met her with a fleet of limos in Red Square.

*So, mama. It's good to see you here in Moscow! Come, we eat!*

She said nothing about the flight, and followed quietly into his limo. He took her to the best restaurant in town, where they were served by an army of waiters. The food was superb, the wine the best money could buy. She said nothing.

*You like the dinner? Come. We fly to my Dacha for drinks.*

The chopper picked them up and delivered them to the steps of a magnificent building, secluded in the outskirts of the city. Waiters in white coats were waiting, and proceeded to serve them with the best Cognac and liquor available.

They sat sipping on the porch, looking out over the view.

*So, mama. You don't say anything. Aren't you proud of your little Miki? Haven't I done well?*

She turned to him and replied in a quiet voice.

*Miki, baby. Is wonderful time I have here. Helicopters are so grand to fly in. Food is best I have ever tasted. And this, a dacha? This is more glorious than anything I could imagine.*

*Yes, Miki. Is wonderful. I am happy for you. But Miki, Baby. What if the communists return!*

{:-) User wears a toupee

## ANOTHER GENIE JOKE

<watmath!ulysses!houdi!jld?>
Jeff David

heard it, laugh

This guy was out playing his weekly round of golf when he hit a shot into the trap off the 11th green. So he pulls out his sand wedge and takes a swing at the ball only to hit something metallic underneath. Being curious, he digs away the sand only to find what looks like Aladdin's Lamp. It's kind of dirty, so he takes out his golf towel to clean it off. All of a sudden... POOF! ... a genie appears from the lamp and says,

*"Sir, you have freed me from the lamp! For this I will grant you 3 wishes!"*

The man thinks for a moment and says, *"You know, I have everything I could possibly want. Give the wishes to someone else."* He quickly putts out and leaves for the 12th tee.

The genie is flabbergasted. *"To think that someone in this world could feel so fulfilled that he could pass up not just 1 but 3 wishes! I know what I'll do. To reward him, I'll grant him 3 things without him knowing. Now lets see. What does every man want? Money! He will have all the money he can use. Power! Every man wants that. And what else? ... Sex! All that he wants."*

A couple of weeks later the man is coming toward the 11th green and there is the genie - sunning himself in the trap.

Genie: (feeling smug) *"Hey. How's it going?"*

Man: *"Couldn't be better. Last week I raised over $1,000,000 and gave the most spellbinding and effective talk of my life. It looks like I'm gaining more influence among my peers and superiors. Things are great."*

Genie: *"If you don't mind me asking, how's your sex life?"*

Man: *"It's great. I've had two women in the last two weeks."*

Genie: (looking puzzled) *"TWO women? That's not very good!"*

Man: *"It is if you're a priest in a small parish!"*

**}:-( Toupee in an updraft**

## THE BAR BET

eddie@pur-ee.UUCP (Mr. X)
Ed Nieters, Purdue University

*(It's an oldie, but a goodie.)*

There was this guy who went into a bar. He went up to the bartender and said, *"Bartender, are you a bettin' man?"*

The bartender replied, *"Certainly! I'm ALWAYS a bettin' man!"* To which the man said, *"I'll bet you $50 that I can lick my right eye."*

The bartender thought about this a while and finally agreed to the bet. The man reached up and pulled out his glass right eye and licked it. The bartender groaned and begrudgingly gave the man his $50 telling him to leave his bar.

A week or so later, the same man appeared in the bar. He went up to the bartender and said, *"Bartender, are you still a bettin' man?"* The bartender replied, *"Certainly! I told you I'm ALWAYS a bettin' man!"* To which the man said, *"I'll bet you $100 that I can bite my left eye."*

Well, the bartender thought he had him on this one! There was no way that he had TWO glass eyes so the bartender agreed. The man reached up to his mouth, pulled out his dentures and clicked them on his left eye. The bartender moaned and paid the man his $100 telling him to get out of his bar.

A week or so later, the same man ventured into the bar again. He went up to the bartender and said, *"Bartender, are you still a bettin' man?"* The bartender said, although with a little caution this time, *"Certainly! I told you I'm ALWAYS a bettin' man!"* To which the man said, *"Give me a shot of whiskey."* The bartender poured the man a shot and he drank it down. Slamming the glass on the bar he said, *"I'll bet you $500 that you can spin me around on this bar stool and I can piss in that glass right where it lays and not miss a drop."*

Well, the bartender's eyes lit up. Here was one time that he was certain that he would win! *"Agreed!"* he cried. Coming out from around the bar, he grabbed onto the man's bar stool and spun it as hard as he could.

Well, the man just let loose and piss flew EVERYPLACE! Not so much as one drop even came close to the glass and the bartender was soaked. When he was done, the bartender was laughing and laughing and holding out his hand. The man pulled out his wallet and gave him his $500. But the bartender was puzzled and as he was wiping off his face, he asked the man, *"Why did you bet me $500 that you could piss in that shot glass on the bar when you had to have known there wasn't any possible way to do it??"*

The man just smiled and told him, *"You may have won $500 off me but I bet that guy over in the corner $10,000 that I could piss all over you and your bar and you would just laugh!"*

---

**:-[ User is a Vampire**

---

## COLLECTION PLATE

jxd9391@ritcv.UUCP (Jim Demitriou)
Rochester Institute of Technology, Rochester, NY                    heard it, laugh

The Mafia was looking for a new man to make weekly collections from all the private businesses that they were 'protecting'. Feeling the heat from the police force, they decide to use a deaf person for this job ; if he were to get caught, he wouldn't be able to communicate to the police what he was doing.

Well, on his first week, the deaf collector picks up over $40,000. He gets greedy, decides to keep the money and stashes it in a safe place. The Mafia soon realizes that their collection is late, and sends some of their hoods after the deaf collector.

The hoods find the deaf collector and ask him where the money is. The deaf collector can't communicate with them, so the Mafia drags the guy to an interpreter.

The Mafia hood says to the interpreter, *"Ask him where da money is."* The interpreter signs, *"Where's the money?"*

The deaf replies, *"I don't know what you're talking about."*

The interpreter tells the hood, *"He says he doesn't know what you're talking about"*

The hood pulls out a .38 and places it in the ear of the deaf collector. *"NOW ask him where the money is."*

The interpreter signs, *"Where is the money?"*

The deaf replies, *"The $40,000 is in a tree stump in Central Park."*

The interpreter's eyes light up and says to the hood, *"He says he still doesn't know what you're talking about, and doesn't think you have the balls to pull the trigger."*

---

## ONE OF MY PERSONAL FAVORITES

john@geac.UUCP (John Henshaw)

The little blue rock next to that twinkly star.

sidesplit, heard it

Scenario: A bishop (B) and a rabbi (R) are sharing a train compartment. After a short while, the two men of the cloth start relating some of their past life experiences...

(General conversation...)

B: *So tell me, rabbi, have you ever actually tasted ham?*

R: *Well yes, in fact. Once when I was very young and daring, I tried it. But only the once...*

(short pause)

R: *So tell me bishop, have you ever ... enjoyed the comforts of a young woman?*

B: *Well, ahem, yes... before I took my vows, mind you, when I was not so old and not so wise...*

[another short pause]

R: *Zo, it's better than ham, hmm?*

---

**:-E User is a bucktoothed Vampire**

---

## SECRET POLICEMAN'S BALL

wall@tilde.UUCP (Raj Wall)

Raj Wall, Texas Instruments

heard it, chuckle

*From London Times via Car and Driver:*

Comrade Gorbachev is being driven from his dacha to Moscow and is in a hurry. He is getting irritated with the slowness of his driver. *"Can't you go any faster?"* he says angrily. *"I have to obey the speed limits,"* says the driver.

Finally Gorbachev orders the driver into the back and takes the wheel. Sure enough a patrol car soon pulls them over. The senior officer orders the junior to go write up the ticket. But the junior officer comes back and says he can't give them a ticket, the person in the car is too important.

*"Well, who is it?"* the senior officer asks.

*"I didn't recognize him,"* says the junior officer, *"but Comrade Gorbachev is his chauffeur."*

## HOW MANY BEANS MAKE THREE?

txt@edsdrd.UUCP (Tri Tran-Viet)
EDS Research, Troy, MI 48007-7019

funny, heard it

While going through his wife's dresser drawers, a farmer discovered three soybeans and an envelope containing $30 in cash. The farmer confronted his wife, and when asked about the curious items, she confessed:

*"Over the years, I haven't been completely faithful to you."*

*"When I did fool around, I put a soybean in the drawer to remind myself of my indiscretion,"* she explained.

The farmer admitted that he had not always been faithful either, and therefore, was inclined to forgive and forget a few moments of weakness in his wife.

*"I'm curious though,"* he said, *"Where did the thirty dollars come from?"*

*"Oh that,"* his wife replied, *"Well, when soybeans hit ten dollars a bushel, I sold out!"*

## ADAM & EVE

ray@isc.intel.com (Ray Asbury)

sexist, offense=men, chuckle, heard it

God one day decided he ought to check in with Adam to see how things were going.

*"Adam....How are things going?"*

*Adam replies that he considers himself quite fortunate to be living in such a beautiful and peaceful place but he did have a couple of questions to ask, if the Lord didn't mind, of course.*

*"No problem,"* said the Lord, *"Ask away"*

*"Well Lord, I was wondering why you made Eve so beautiful? Not that I'm complaining, mind you."*

*"Adam, I made Eve so beautiful so that you would like her."*

*"Oh, well yes, I do like her very much. Thank you Lord. You made her so beautiful, but why is it then that you made her so stupid?"*

*"Well Adam, I had to make sure she liked you too!"*

**:-F User is a bucktoothed Vampire with one tooth missing**

## NUN OF THAT HERE

demasi@paisano.UUCP (Michael C. De Masi)

AT&T Communications. Fairfax, VA — sexual, offense=Catholics, rot13, swearing

A guy gets on a bus and notices a nun sitting over in a corner. Through her heavy head piece he just spots a glimmer of her face. Gorgeous! She moves, and her vestments cannot hide the fact she has a truly phenomenal body. The guy gets more and more excited until he finally approaches the nun and tells *"Sister, I don't normally do this sort of thing, but I think I love you. Can we get together some time?"*

The nun leaves the bus in a huff.

Later as the guy is about to leave the bus himself, the bus driver asks the guy if he was the one who was bothering the nun. The guy again apologizes, explaining once again that he seldom did this sort of thing, but the bus driver says: *"No, don't apologize, I was checking her out myself. In fact, let me do you a favor. Did you see where she got off? There's a little park there, and every day she goes there to pray at the same time. Go there tomorrow, and maybe....."*

The guy thanks him and leaves.

Sure enough, the guy goes to the park and there's the little nun in a secluded spot by some trees. He goes off into the bushes, and comes back a few minutes later in a long white robe, a long blond wig with beard and a crown of thorns. The nun is flabbergasted, and asks what she can do for him. He says that every couple of thousand years, he likes to come back to earth to get laid. The nun says that she'd love to help him, but that she was on her period, and would the back door be OK?

He says fine, and they commence their activities.

A few minutes into it, he is suddenly overcome with a blast of guilt, and says, panting, *"Sister, I have to tell you something. I'm not really Jesus, I'm actually the guy who was annoying you on the bus yesterday."*

The nun says, *"Oh, that's OK. In fact, I'm not really a nun. I'm actually the bus driver."*

## MAKING A MOUNTAIN OUT OF A MOEL

kane@batcomputer.UUCP (Yana Kane-Esrig)                    funny

A tourist in a strange town notices that her watch is broken. She starts looking for a repair shop. After a long and frustrating search she finds herself in an area where many shop signs are in Hebrew. Finally, she notices that one of the stores has all kinds of clocks and watches ticking merrily in the window. She walks into the shop and puts her watch on the counter in front of the proprietor.

Tourist: *"Would you please repair this watch."*

Proprietor: *"Madam, I cannot repair your watch."*

T: *"But why not? It is an ordinary model."*

P: *"Madam, I do not repair watches. I am a moel, I perform circumcisions."*

T (irritated): *"Then why on earth do you have all these clocks in your window?"*

P: *"Well, and what should I have in my window?"*

## AUSTRALIA

sater@cs.vu.nl (Hans van Staveren)                    chuckle

Some years ago an Englishman on a plane to Australia was handed one of these cards to fill in, in normal Commonwealth style. After the standard ones, like name, nationality, passport number, etc.. he got to one that asked:

*"Have you ever been imprisoned?"*

After thinking about that for some time he entered: *"I didn't know it was still a requirement."*

## NEWFIE GOES INTO A BAR

w-colinp@microsof.UUCP (Colin)                    anti-anti-ethnic, chuckle

Two guys are sitting in a bar swapping Newfie jokes. A Newfie comes in, and, after listening for a bit, contributes one of his own:

*"How do you get a Newfie girl pregnant?"*

The two guys are stumped. *"I dunno."*

*"Gee, and you say Newfies are stupid!"*

## A MAN WITH A PROBLEM
daryl@hpcllla.UUCP (Daryl Odnert)
Hewlett-Packard, California Language Lab

sexual, chuckle

A middle aged businessman goes to see his physician.

"Doctor, I've got this problem," the man says. "My secretary, she loves to give blow jobs. Every morning when I get to work I get a blow job. She gives me a quick one before I leave for lunch. And before I leave work at the end of the day she really works me over."

"So what seems to be the problem?" the doctor asked.

"Well, you see, my wife is a nymphomaniac," the man continued. "I service her every morning when we get up. I go home for a quick half hour every day at lunch and then we have a marathon session each night before we go to sleep."

"I still don't know what your problem is," said the doctor.

"You see Doc, every time I masturbate I get these dizzy spells."

**:-7 User just made a wry statement**

## FUNNY WHO YOU MEET
vel@umd5.umd.edu (Daniel Fivel)
University of Maryland, College Park

chuckle

Elderly woman meets elderly gentleman on the street.

Her: *Aren't you Ed Filby? I haven't seen you in thirty-years.*

Him: *That's me.*

Her: *You look pretty good - but a little pale. Where you been?*

Him: *Been in jail actually.*

Her: *Really! What did you do?*

Him: *Well, I killed my wife. I chopped her up in little pieces and put her in the garbage disposal.*

Her: *Oh!... so you're not married!*

## WISDOM OF THE GODS

hmm@laura.irb.informatik.uni-dortmund.de
Hans-Martin Mosner

swearing, chuckle

A man walks along a lonely beach. Suddenly he hears a deep voice: DIG !

He looks around: nobody's there.  I am having hallucinations, he thinks. Then he hears the voice again: I SAID, DIG !

So he starts to dig in the sand with his bare hands, and after some inches, he finds a small chest with a rusty lock.

The deep voice says: OPEN !

OK, the man thinks, let's open the thing.  He finds a rock with which to destroy the lock, and when the chest is finally open, he sees a lot of gold coins.

The deep voice says: TO THE CASINO !

Well the casino is only a few miles away, so the man takes the chest and walks to the casino.

The deep voice says: ROULETTE !

So he changes all the gold into a huge pile of roulette tokens and goes to one of the tables, where the players gaze at him with disbelief.

The deep voice says: 27 !

He takes the whole pile and drops it at the 27.  The table nearly bursts. Everybody is quiet when the croupier throws the ball.

The ball stays at the 26.

The deep voice says: SHIT !

## HOW WRONG CAN A GUY BE?

beshers@cs.columbia.edu (Clifford Beshers)
Columbia University Computer Science Department

funny, sexual

*(I remember this from a Playboy issue of many years ago.)*

A man picks up a young woman in a bar and convinces her to come back to his hotel. When they are relaxing afterwards, he asks, *"Am I the first man you ever made love to?"* She looks at him thoughtfully for a second before replying. *"You might be,"* she says. *"Your face looks familiar."*

## ANSWER TO QUESTION ON NUDISM

al@gtx.com (Alan Filipski)
GTX Corporation, Phoenix

original, funny, sexual references

*In article @ucbvax.BERKELEY.EDU amorando@euler.berkeley.edu (David Ashley) writes:*

I would like to ask a question that has bothered me ever since I heard about nude places like beaches, parks and whatnot.

What if you are a guy and you get a hard on. Do you try and cover it up (don't ask ME how) or does everyone just take it for granted and politely ignore it? Or do nudists say that the problem never comes up due to self-control?

This is a common question among newcomers to nudist activities. In practice, it is nothing to worry about. What usually happens is something like this:

You get an erection, somebody notices, points at you and yells, "Hey, look at the hard-on on that guy" or, "Look at that guy trying to hide his hard-on." Then everyone gathers around, pointing and laughing. If you try to run away, they all follow you. People start taking pictures. Eventually, some mesomorph/homophobe thinks he catches you looking at his girlfriend/self and beats the hell out of you. After this happens two or three times, you get conditioned to always go limp when you see a naked body.

No problem.

> :-* User just ate something sour

## BLIND LUCK

eacj@tcgould.TN.CORNELL.EDU (Julian Vrieslander)

chuckle

A young woman has just undressed to step into the shower when the doorbell rings. She goes to the door and says, *"Who is it?"*

*"Blind man,"* comes the reply.

So instead of going back to the bathroom for her robe, she opens the door.

*"Hmmm.. nice body, lady. Where do you want the blinds?"*

## IT'S NOT THE MEAT
rostamia@umbc3.umbc.edu (Rouben Rostamian)                     funny, sexual

*(Source: Playboy Magazine)*

A Frenchman and an Italian were seated next to an American in an overseas flight. After a few cocktails, the men began discussing their home lives.

*"Last night I made love to my wife four times,"* the Frenchman bragged, "and this morning she made me delicious crepes and she told me how much she adored me."

*"Ah, last night I made love to my wife six times,"* the Italian responded, "and this morning she made me a wonderful omelet and told me she could never love another man."

When the American remained silent, the Frenchman smugly asked, *"And how many times did you make love to your wife last night?"*

*"Once,"* he replied.

*"Only once?"* the Italian arrogantly snorted. *"And what did she say to you this morning?"*

*"Don't stop."*

**:-)~ User drools**

## MEMORIAL DAY
grazier@newton.physics.purdue.edu (Kevin R. Grazier)                     funny

*As told to me by a friend in the British Army:*

A British officer spotted a "busker" (street singer/bum) at the bottom of the escalator of the London Underground. The busker had a sign which read: *"VETERAN SOLDIER OF THE FALKLANDS WAR."* The officer thought, *"Poor chap, I was there and it was awful!"* Feeling sorry for a fellow veteran, the officer took 20 pounds out of his wallet and gave it to the busker. The officer was then greeted with a hearty: *"Gracias, Senor!!"*

**:-~) User has a cold**

## A DIFFERENT POLISH JOKE

euatdt@euas11g.ericsson.se (Torsten Dahlkvist)

funny

*This one may be old on the net (I certainly heard it a number of years ago), but in case you haven't heard it before, here goes a story the Polish tell about Russians...*

A Russian party-official arrives late at night to his hotel (in Russia). He is not surprised to find that his reservation has been mislaid but he is more than a little peeved that his status in the party isn't enough to get him a good room anyway. However, the clerk insists, the only bed they have left is the fourth bunk in a 4-bed dorm— he'll have to make do with that. The Russian grumbles but eventually he picks up his suitcase and heads for the dorm. On his way, he meets a chamber-maid and thinking he might as well try to make friends with his room-mates, he asks her to bring them four cups of tea.

As he enters the dorm, he finds that the other three guests are Polish, they are having a fairly wild party and they're very drunk. They also ignore him totally from the moment he enters. After sitting there for several minutes, he realizes he can't stand them anymore and decides to pull a joke on them. He stands up, grasps a floor lamp and speaking into the light-bulb as if it were a microphone he says:

*"Comrade Colonel, we would like four cups of tea to our room immediately!"* The Poles stare at him in disbelief, which turns to horror as the chamber-maid knocks on the door and delivers the tea a few minutes later. In about 30 seconds the Poles have all packed their bags and fled the hotel. Our Russian gets the entire room to himself. He sleeps very soundly.

The next morning, however, as he's checking out and is about to leave, the desk-clerk calls after him:

*"By the way, Sir, the Comrade Colonel said to tell you he appreciated your little joke last night!"*

## THIS JOKE QUACKS ME UP

john%hpdsla@hp-sde.sde.hp.com (John Fereira)

meta-joke, chuckle, sexual?

A duck walks into a pharmacy waddles up to the prescription counter and rings the bell. The pharmacist walks up and asks, *"Can I help you?"* The duck replies, *"Yes, I would like a box of condoms."* *"Why certainly,"* says the pharmacist, *"will that be cash or would you like me to put it on your bill?"* The duck answers, *"What kind of duck do you think I am?"*

`:* Kisses`

## FERRY TALE

2014_5001@uwovax.uwo.ca (A.R. PRUSS)                    funny, sexual, stereotypes

A young French girl was visiting New York when her cash funds run dry and her visa expired. She met a sailor who agreed to stow her aboard his ship that was about to sail. Every day he would bring her food and drink and in return all she had to do was give him a bit of love. Lacking much choice, the girl agreed.

And so everyday, the sailor brought some food and would get some loving in return. This went on for several weeks until the captain saw the sailor sneaking around with a tray of food and the whole affair was uncovered. The captain felt obliged to apologize to the girl:

*"I'm very sorry about all that has happened to you, but you have to admit the sailor is smart. Do you know you're on the Staten Island Ferry?"*

`:'-) User is so happy, s/he is crying`

## SAFETY

peghiny@milpnd.enet.dec.com (DEC Joke Exchange)                    sexual, chuckle

The pretty teacher was concerned with one of her eleven-year-old students. Taking him aside after class one day, she asked, *"George, why has your school work been so poor lately?"*

*"I'm in love,"* the boy replied.

Holding back an urge to smile, she asked, *"With whom?"*

*"With you,"* he said.

*"But George,"* she said gently, *"don't you see how silly that is? It's true that I would like a husband of my own someday. But I don't want a child."*

*"Oh, don't worry,"* the boy said reassuringly, *"I'll use a rubber."*

`:-@ User is screaming`

# A PARATROOPER'S FIRST JUMP

garison@prism.TMC.COM (Gary E. Piatt)

explicit sexual, funny

*(I heard this from my stepson, who says that it was running rampant in the barracks while he was in the Army...)*

A young man joined the Army and signed up with the paratroopers. He went though the standard training, completed the practice jumps from higher and higher structures, and finally went to take his first jump from an airplane. The next day, he called home to his father to tell him the news.

*"So, did you jump?"* the father asked.

*"Well, let me tell you what happened. We got up in the plane, and the sergeant opened up the door and asked for volunteers. About a dozen men got up and just walked out of the plane!"*

*"Is that when you jumped?"* asked the father.

*"Um, not yet. Then the sergeant started to grab the other men one at a time and throw them out the door."*

*"Did you jump then?"* asked the father.

*"I'm getting to that. Every one else had jumped, and I was the last man left on the plane. I told the sergeant that I was too scared to jump. He told be to get off the plane or he'd kick my butt."*

*"So, did you jump?"*

*"Not then. He tried to push me out of the plane, but I grabbed onto the door and refused to go. Finally he called over the Jump Master. The Jump Master is this great big guy, about six-foot five, and 250 pounds. He said to me, 'Boy, are you gonna jump or not?' I said, 'No, sir. I'm too scared.' So the Jump Master pulled down his zipper and took his penis out. I swear, it was about ten inches long and as big around as a baseball bat! He said, 'Boy, either you jump out that door, or I'm sticking this little baby up your ass.'"*

*"So, did you jump?"* asked the father.

*"Well, a little, at first."*

# ONE MORE BANJO JOKE. . .

mary%zaphod@gargoyle.uchicago.edu

musician stereotypes?, chuckle

Got this one from my sister's boyfriend, Cajun accordionist extraordinaire, after he sold me his banjo:

Q. What's the difference between a runover skunk and a runover banjo player?

A. *The skunk was on its way to a gig.*

## BEAR BELLS

c-jonw@microsoft.UUCP (Jon Waite, Seattle)                                                           chuckle

A guy walks into this sporting goods store in Alaska, immediately spies a rather haggard-looking old salt of a store clerk sitting by the cash register.

*"Hear ya got a lotta' bears 'round here?"*

*"Yep,"* answers the clerk.

*"Big bears?"*

*"Yep."*

*"Mean bears?"*

*"Yep."*

*"Black bears?"*

*"Yep."*

*"GRIZZLIES???!"*

*"Yep."*

*"Got any bear bells?"*

*"What's dat?"*

*"You know, them little dingle-bells ya put on yer backpack so bears know yer in the perimeter so's they can runs away ..."*

*"Yep. Over yonder ..."*

*"Great. I'll take one fer black bears, and one fer grizzlies. Say, how'd you know if yer in black bear country anyway?"*

*"Look fer scat."*

*"Oh. Well, how how'd you know if there's GRIZZLIES????!"*

*"Look fer scat."*

*"You just said that!"*

*"Yeah. But grizzly scat's different."*

*"Well now, just what's IN grizzly scat that's different?"*

*"Bear bells."*

---

**:^) User has a broken nose**

---

## QUALIFYING EXAM FOR INCOME TAX FORM DESIGNERS

rost@decwrl.UUCP (Randi Rost)                                    funny

Read each question thoroughly. Answer all questions. Time limit is four hours.

1. HISTORY. Describe the history of all religions from their earliest origins to the present day. Prove which is best in a manner that will convince all other religions.

2. MEDICINE. You will be provided with a razor blade, a piece of gauze, and a bottle of scotch. Remove your own appendix. Do not suture until your work has been inspected. You will have fifteen minutes.

3. PUBLIC SPEAKING. 2500 riot-crazed aborigines will be turned loose in the classroom with you. Calm them. You may use any ancient language except Latin or Greek.

4. BIOLOGY. Create life. Estimate the differences in subsequent human culture if this form of life had developed 500 million years earlier, with special attention to the probable effects on our next election. Show who would have been our next President and why.

5. MUSIC. Write a piano concerto. Orchestrate it and perform it with flute and drum. You will find a piano under your seat.

6. PSYCHOLOGY. Based on your knowledge of their works, evaluate the political stability, degree of adjustment, and repressed frustrations of each of the following: Alexander of Aphrodisias, Ramsesall, Gregory of Nicoa, and Hammurabi. Support your evaluations with quotations from each man's work, making appropriate references. It is not necessary to translate.

7. SOCIOLOGY. Estimate the sociological problems which might accompany the end of the world. Construct a full-scale experiment to test your theory.

8. MANAGEMENT SCIENCE. Define management. Define science. How do they relate? Why? Create a generalized algorithm that can be used to optimize all managerial decisions. Design the systems interface and prepare all software necessary to program this algorithm on whatever computer may be selected by the examiner.

9. ENGINEERING. The disassembled parts of a high-powered rifle will be placed on your desk. You will also find an instruction manual, printed in Swahili. In ten minutes a hungry Bengal tiger will be admitted into the room. Take whatever action you feel appropriate. Be prepared to justify your decision.

10. ECONOMICS. Develop a realistic plan for refinancing the national debt. Trace the possible effects of your plan on the wave theory of light and on the overcrowding of citizens band radio channels.

11. POLITICAL SCIENCE. Pick up the phone on the desk beside you and start World War III. Report at length on its socio-political effects, if any.

12. EPISTEMOLOGY. Take a position for or against the truth. Prove the validity of your position.

13. PHYSICS. Explain the nature of matter. Include in your answer an evaluation of the impact of mathematics on science, plus the possible effect of electromagnetic radiation on global pollution and on the love life of radar operators who spend long periods in that environment.

14. PHILOSOPHY. Sketch the development of human thought; estimate its significance. Compare this with the development of other kinds of thought.

15. GENERAL KNOWLEDGE. Describe everything you know in detail. Be objective and specific.

16. EXTRA CREDIT. Define the universe. Give three examples.

---

:-Q User is a smoker

---

# Chapter Three
# Topical Jokes

The electronic networks are the fastest medium that exists for the printed word. While ordinary joke collections would not specialize in jokes on the latest current events, **rec.humor.funny** revels in them. Some of them, of course, are dated, but I've included a chapter of the best of the topical jokes from the years covered in this volume.

---

### O.J. SIMPSON DIGEST
cz23+@andrew.cmu.edu (Clay R. Zambo)                                   topical, chuckle

Day Care?
Heard on an otherwise dull AM radio talk show this morning (no, I was looking for the news!):
CALLER: I just saw a CNN update on the O. J. Simpson case. Michael Jackson has volunteered to take care of the kids.

drhodes@hercules.win.net (Dylan Rhodes)
If an ex-football player had to kill his wife, why couldn't it have been Frank Gifford?

DSROGER@saix367.sandia.gov (Rogers, Scott)
OJ calls a limo service and requests a limo.
The dispatcher tells Mr. Simpson *"Yes sir Mr. Simpson we have a limo for you, but it will be a 45 minute wait."*

OJ replies, *"Great, I have some time to kill."*
Source: Co-worker

foster@seismo.css.gov (Glen Foster)

This one is original and came to me while watching the OJ debacle at my favorite watering hole Friday night:

Q. What's worse than being married to John Bobbit?

*A. Being divorced from OJ Simpson.*

bhatia@louie.udel.edu (Sunita Kumari Bhatia)

Knock, knock.
Who's there?
OJ.
OJ who?
Congratulations! You're on the jury!
[Ed: this joke was submitted by more than 20 people]

## OJ AND THE WORLD CUP

nwarmenh@reed.edu (Nic Warmenhoven)

My father wrote this one:

What amazes me about OJ's pre-trial hearing was that the defense NEVER mentioned that both Nicole Simpson and Ron Goldman scored own goals against Colombia! I mean, you'd think...

**:-c Bummed out smiley**

## OJ'S LATEST ALIBI

pd411x@unix1.circ.gwu.edu (P.J. Geraghty)

Seems OJ will finally beat the rap, as he has an airtight alibi...
. . .He was in a Denny's waiting to be served...

Q. What's the question they're asking in the California penal system?

*A. Who gets to have O.J. for breakfast?*

## EMAIL TO THE CHIEF

nweaver@soda.berkeley.edu (Nicholas C. Weaver)    topical, chuckle, computer

(Overheard in the Computer Science Undergraduate Association office)

Everyone on the net by now knows that mail to the President can be sent to president@whitehouse.gov, and that mail to the Vice President should be addressed to vice-president@whitehouse.gov. However, most people don't realize that mail to Hillary Clinton should be addressed to root@whitehouse.gov.

## NO, BAD TEETH

Martin.Soques@amd.com (Martin Soques)    topical, chuckle

Saw this on our local paper yesterday:

Q. What do you get when you cross a crooked lawyer and a crooked politician?

A. Chelsea.

## WORKERS OF THE WORLD..ABANDON SHIP!

rewing@apple.com (Richard Ewing)    topical, smirk

As told by Diane Sawyer on Prime Time Live, from a joke currently circulating inside the eastern bloc:

Q. What's the difference between the United States and Eastern European countries?

A. The United States still has a communist party.

:-v Talking head smiley

## MODERN TIMES

jans@stammer.GVS.TEK.COM (Jan Steinman)    topical, funny

Q. What's the difference between the 90's and the 50's?

A. In the 80's, a man walks into a drugstore and states loudly, "I'd like some condoms," then whispers, "and some cigarettes."

## THE POPE AND GARY HART

jsp@b.gp.cs.cmu.edu (John Pieper)
Carnegie-Mellon University, CS/RI

sidesplit, offense=Catholics

(I have been told that this joke is sacriligious. Caveat Emptor.)
*Ok, so here it is:*

It so happens that the Pope and Gary Hart died at the same time. There was a mix-up, and the Pope was sent to Hell and Hart went to Heaven. Of course, Satan immediately realized the error. He was quite displeased, so he set about to rectify the situation at once. Nevertheless, relations between Heaven and Hell being what they are, it took a full day for the trade to be arranged. When the Pope heard he was going to Heaven after all, he was much relieved, but being the caring soul he was, he was worried that Gary would be upset at the change. So when they met halfway, the Pope said,

*"Mr. Hart, I know you must be very disappointed, but you know I did live eighty years of a clean life bound to God, so that I could claim my Reward and kneel at the feet of the Virgin."*

And Gary, grinning, replies, *"Well, Your Holiness, I'm afraid you're a little too late for that!"*

---

**:-] Smiley blockhead**

---

## SOME TAMMY BAKKER HUMOUR

brad@ut-sally.UUCP (blumenthal @ home with the armadillos)
U. Texas CS Dept., Austin, Texas

chuckle, topical

In article <3540020@hpfcdt.HP.COM> ajs@hpfcdt.HP.COM (Alan Silverstein) writes:

Here's the Tammy Bakker ski report:
  One inch base, and two inches of powder.
  .. and lots of long lift lines.

Q. By the way... why is it spelled with two 'k's?

A. *Because three would be too obvious.*

*Thanks to Rob Shook.*

## HIS FINAL TEXT

clf@cblpf.ATT.COM (Chris, x3660)
AT&T Bell Laboratories - Columbus, Ohio

laugh, topical

Q. What is Jim Baker now preaching?

A. *Thou shalt not put thy rod in thy staff.*

**:-{ Smiley variation on a theme**

## JESUS LOVES THE LITTLE CHILDREN

commgrp@silver.bacs.indiana.edu
The Unix(R) Connection, Dallas, Texas

topical, funny

Q. How did Jim Bakker initially meet Tammy?

A. *They were both dating Jimmy Swaggart.*

**:-} ditto**

## GORBACHEV AND BUSH

adam@media-lab.media.mit.edu (Adam Glass)

topical, funny

Told to me by my father, who heard it from his cousin:
Gorbachev is hard at work on his country's budget. His secretary knocks on the door. *"Mr. Secretary, the—"*

*"Not now, I'm busy!"*

*"But..."*

*"Nyet! Come back in two hours."*

Thirty seconds later, she knocks again. *"Mr. Secretary, the phone... you must answer it."*

*"Can't you see I'm working on the budget?! I must have silence. Have them call back tomorrow."*

*"But Mr. Secretary, it's Mr. Bush on the phone. He says he has 5 billion dollars for you, and you don't have to pay any of it back!"*

Gorbachev smiles and picks up the phone. *"Hello, Neil..."*

## COLLECTION OF STOCK MARKET JOKES AFTER THE CRASH
funny@looking.UUCP

1) Submitted by several, first Greg Woods

Q. What's the difference between a pigeon and a stockbroker?

*A. The pigeon can still make a deposit on a BMW.*

2) Submitted by several, first Kyle Adler

These two women were walking through the forest when they hear this voice from under a log. Investigating, the women discovered the voice was coming from a frog:

*"Help me, ladies! I am an investment banker who, through an evil witch's curse, has been transformed into a frog. If one of you will kiss me, I'll be returned to my former state!"*

The first woman took out her purse, grabbed the frog, and stuffed it inside her handbag. The second woman, aghast, screamed, *"Didn't you hear him? If you kiss him, he'll turn into an investment banker?"*

The second woman replied, *"Sure, but these days a talking frog is worth more than an investment banker!"*

3) From Patricia Giencke— and the New York Times

Merrill Lynch has adjusted its investment portfolio: 50% cash and 50% canned goods.

Bumper sticker on Wall Street:
My other Porsche is for sale.

How many investment bankers can you fit in the back of a pickup truck? Only 2 - you have to leave room for the lawn mowers!

I have an uncle down at Wall Street. He used to have a corner on the market. Now he has a market on the corner.

*"Get my broker, Miss Jones."*
*"Yes sir. Stock, or Pawn?"*

4) Some very, very old jokes used in just about all bad times, now applied to the market:

Q. In these busy market times, how can you get the attention of your broker?

*A. Say, "Hey, waiter!"*

Q. How do you get a broker down from a tree?

A. *Cut the rope.*

5) The market may be bad, but I slept like a baby last night. I woke up every hour and cried.

Many have sent jokes about broker suicides. Since there actually were very few, if any, both now and in 1929, these didn't really get much of a laugh. You could also see them all coming down 6th Avenue, so I'm not posting.

---

## DOWN ON THE FARM
steve@raspail.UUCP (Steve Schonberger)                                          funny, topical

I read this in the newspaper where I used to live, the *Lincoln Star*. I am not sure if it was wire service news or a joke, but I know it was not local, because Nebraska doesn't have a lottery. I am not quoting exactly— it appeared a year or so back and I forget the exact words.

Interviewer: *Congratulations on winning the lottery.*

Farmer: *Thank you.*

Interviewer: *Do you have any special plans for spending the money?*

Farmer: *Not really. I'm just gonna keep farming 'til it's gone.*

---

## TAMMY FAYE BAKKER
John R. Snyder (206) 543-7798 <june.cs.washington.edu!jsnyder>                   topical, funny

Q. Did you hear what happened when they took off all of Tammy Faye's makeup?

A. *They found Jimmy Hoffa.*

---

## QUAYLE JOKE
evan@sunrise.COM (Evan Marcus)
Sun Microsystems, NY District Office                                            topical, sexual, laugh

Q. What did Marilyn Quayle say to her husband immediately after sex?

A. *You really are no Jack Kennedy.*

---

## MICHAEL JACKSON
aeusejwd@csuna.UUCP (john dyson)
California State University, Northridge                                    laugh

Q. Why is Michael Jackson's new album entitled "Bad?"
*A. Because he couldn't spell "Pathetic."*

## ANOTHER BY RUSHDIE?
steve@raspail.cdcnet.cdc.com (Steve Schonberger)          topical, funny, offense=Buddhists

This one was posted anonymously to a Minneapolis-Saint Paul area bulletin board system. I edited it a little.

Salman Rushdie plans to release another book soon. It's tentatively titled, "Buddha, You Fat Slob."

[Ed: Reportedly Herb Caen tells a similar joke.]

## A THOUSAND POINTS OF AMNESIA
steven@uts.amdahl.com (Steven Swinkels, Fearless Leader)          topical, funny

(From Carson's monologue)

"I understand the attorneys are having a lot of trouble finding jurors for the Oliver North trial.. They have to locate 12 people that have never heard of the Iran-Contra scandal ...

.. so far, they've only been able to come up with George Bush."

---

**{:-) Smiley with its hair parted in the middle**

---

## AUSTRIA
jimk@iscuva.ISCS.COM (Jim Kendall)
ISC Systems Corporation, Spokane, WA                              heard it, funny

From the David Letterman Show:

WALDHEIMERS disease is what you have when you can't remember you were a Nazi.

## MARCOS
pt@geovision.UUCP (Paul Tomblin)                    sick, funny, topical

I can't understand why Corey Aquino won't allow Ferdinand Marcos back into the country to die.

. . . After all, he let her husband come back into the country to die.

**:-s Smiley after a BIZARRE comment**

## GOOD NEWS, BAD NEWS
jap@cbnews.ATT.COM (James A. Parker)              original, topical, funny

[The following is, as far as I can tell, original with me.]

There's good news and bad news on the investigation of the nuclear missile dropped overboard near Japan:

The good news is that the U.S. Navy is going to scan for signs of excess radiation.

The bad news is that they've hired Fleischmann and Pons to do the testing.

## THE BAR BAT
Fred_Ennis@Compuserve

topical, funny

Three baseball greats were having a beer in a bar.

An attractive woman walked in and Wade Boggs said, *"I wonder if she's alone?"*

Steve Garvey warned, *"Be careful, she's carrying my child!"*

Pete Rose finally piped up and said, *"Wanna Bet?"*

## WHO HAS....
gmw1@cunixd.cc.columbia.edu (Gabe M Wiener)        topical, chuckle

Q: Who has long silky hair, voluptuous tits, and lives in Wisconsin?

A: *Salman Rushdie*

### STEALTH BOMBER BUMPER STICKER

eli@ursa-major.SPDCC.COM                                        topical, funny

From Letterman show:

bumper sticker seen on stealth bomber:

"IF YOU CAN READ THIS,
THEN WE WASTED 50 BILLION BUCKS."

[Ed: Ok, so it's only 32 billion. What's 18B between friends?]

---

**g-) Smiley with pince-nez glasses**

---

### NOCTURNAL RECREATIONAL HABITS OF CALIFORNIA COPS

eps@toaster.sfsu.edu (Eric P. Scott)
San Francisco State University                                 topical, funny

Q. What's the difference between a police officer in San Francisco and a police officer in Los Angeles?

*A. A police officer in San Francisco will dance and have a few drinks when he says he's going out "clubbing."*

### GATES IS BACK

matchmaker@houston.relay.ucm.org                               topical, chuckle

They finally let Chief Gates come back to his job with the LA Police Dept.
He's also introducing some new legislation.
He wants a requirement to have everyone wait 7 days to get a camcorder.

### NEW LAPD MOTTO

david@elroy.jpl.nasa.gov (David Robinson)                      topical, chuckle

LAPD has a new motto: To Protect and Serve, and Treat You Like a King

---

### CORY HITS IT BIG

berman-andrew@yale.UUCP (Andrew P. Berman)                     chuckle

Q. What was Corazon Aquino's happiest hour?

*A. When she found out she had Imelda Marcos' shoe size.*

---

## PRE-GULF WAR JOKES

The Editor                                                    topical, chuckle

The following are some of the better jokes from before the war, some of which can be found in volume III of the *TeleJokeBook*

Q: What did Saddam say to George Bush after he invaded Kuwait?

A: *Read my lips, I'm pulling out of Kuwait.*

If he did pull out it would be *Kuwaitis Interruptus.*

```
*Iraq += *Kuwait;
free(Kuwait);
num_countries- -;
```

Kurt Waldheim met recently with Saddam and said, *"Saddam, I knew Adolf Hitler; Adolf Hitler was a friend of mine, and Saddam, you're no Adolph Hitler."*

Saddam says that if anybody else compares him to Hitler, he'll gas them.

Picture of an Iraqi on a camel viewed through a gunsight. Caption: *"I'd fly 10,000 miles to smoke a camel."*

Picture: Iraqi tank on the desert with a "baby on board" window sticker.

George Bush heard there was a Gulf Crisis, misunderstood, and went to work on his chipping.

Q: What does Saddam want for Thanksgiving?

A: *Turkey.*

## KUWAITI BUSINESS BUMPER STICKER

patti%hose2@uunet.uu.net                                       topical, chuckle

What if Kuwait's main product were broccoli?

## HOW TO REALLY "MAKE MONEY FAST"

jeff@digicomp.com (Jeff Carroll)                               topical, chuckle

In order to raise capital for his presidential library, I hear they've installed a juke-box next to Nixon's grave.

## CHARGE

vaughan%henri@hub.ucsb.edu (George S. Vaughan)    topical, funny

From the Osgood File, on the radio:

Regarding the Persian Gulf, what's the difference between the US and France, and Japan and Germany?

The US and France yelled, *"Charge!"* and waved their rifles.

Japan and Germany yelled, *"Charge!"* and waved their credit cards.

## MILK FACTORY

ch@dce.ie (Charles Bryant)    topical, funny, pun

Gulf war latest: Americans announce that the "milk factory" was in fact a centre for exterminating curds.

## THIS ONE BOMBED IN BAGHDAD

C.ROCK2@genie.com    topical, chuckle

Heard this one at the office. *"Why are there no WalMarts in Baghdad? Because there is a Target on every corner!"*

## STANFORD HONOR CODE

fruitbat@leland.stanford.edu (Thomas Fruchterman)    original, funny, topical

[Ed: Honourable Mention in the Original Comedy Awards.]

I was taking a take-home exam in a class at Stanford. The instructions said *"You are expected to abide by the Stanford Code in your actions."* So I billed the federal government for remodeling my house.

## THEFT IN EAST BERLIN

pk@caen.engin.umich.edu (Payman Khalili)    topical, chuckle

I heard this from a friend of mine. I don't know where it originated.

An East Berliner going to a bar parks his bike next to the wall.
He comes back. There's no bicycle... and no wall!

## IRAQ AROUND THE CLOCK (TOP TEN LISTS)

HAUSMANN_MADDI@tandem.com (Maddi Hausmann)
Tandem Computers, Cupertino, CA   topical, original, funny

[Ed: Honourable Mention in the Original Comedy Awards.]

TOP TEN REASONS Saddam Hussein didn't pull troops out of Kuwait by midnight, 15 January:

10. Busy preparing quarterly estimated tax payments

9. Figured out Bush never said January 15th, <u>1991</u>

8. Tried to but entire Iraqi army sunbathing on Kuwaiti beach

7. Already answered Tommy Lasorda's request to "Give Ultra Slim Fast a Week"

6. Out shopping at Macy's White Sale

5. Didn't want to violate sanctity of Martin Luther King Holiday

4. No one told him the hostages were let go already

3. Glued to television set seeing who won Publishers Clearinghouse Sweepstakes

2. In midst of serious negotiations with Lockheed over "invalid during act of war" clause in missile warranty

1. Still trying to meet midnight, 15 January deadline for tendering NCR shares to AT&T.

## SADDAM HUSSEIN'S LAW DEGREE

bill@emx.utexas.edu (Bill Jefferys)   topical, original, funny

ABC's Good Morning America show interviewed an expert on military history, who said something that I didn't know, namely, that Saddam Hussein actually has a law degree. He went on to point out that the degree was granted under somewhat unusual circumstances: Saddam Hussein was accompanied by two heavily armed guards into the examination room, and apparently it was felt that there was no need to grade the exam.

Upon hearing this, my first thought was that Saddam had cheated. But the expert quickly pointed out that the incident demonstrates that Saddam really has an excellent understanding of Iraqi law.

## THE TRIALS OF SADDAM

A.NEFT@genie.com                                                    topical, funny

There is some good news and bad news about Saddam Hussein's war crimes trial. The good news is that President Bush will try him. The bad news is, the trial will be held before the Senate Ethics Committee.

## SADDAM'S TOP TEN WITHDRAWAL CONDITIONS

bakken@cs.arizona.edu (Dave Bakken)          topical, funny, original, national stereotypes

Saddam Hussein's Top Ten Conditions for Quitting Kuwait

10) Syria must give control of Lebanon back to Lebanon, which must in turn give control back to Phoenicia.

9) The US must sell Alaska back to Russia and the Louisiana Purchase back to France.

8) Saudi Arabia must pay for all the Scuds that were fired at it to liberate Palestine.

7) The Pope must convert to Islam (or at least Baathism).

6) All Israeli Jews must tread water in the Mediterranean Sea for 40 years.

5) Spain must give back much of its land to the Moors.

4) Kuwait must reimburse Iraq for the costs of transporting Iraqi troops into Kuwait and Kuwaiti goods into Iraq.

3) The Kurds must repay Iraq's expenses incurred while dropping poison gas on them.

2) King Fahd and Presidents Mubarak and Assad must have a mud wrestling match, with only the last man remaining in the ring being spared from execution.

*And his most important condition:*

1) George Bush must apologize to the UN General Assembly in drag.

**:-d Lefty smiley razzing you**

## SAUDI NATIONAL ANTHEM
herlihy@crl.dec.com

*topical, smirk*

From the New York Times:

Q. What's the new Saudi national anthem?

A. *Onward Christian Soldiers.*

## COMING FOR TO CARRY ME HOME
J.KOBLEUR@genie.com (KRAFTY)

*topical, pun, chuckle*

Q. Did you hear that the L.A. Lakers drafted Saddam Hussein?

A. *Yes, they wanted someone who could shoot over Jordan.*

## IRAQI BUMPER STICKERS
J.EVERETT7@genie.com (gumball)

*topical, chuckle, iraq*

"My dad went to Kuwait and all he brought me
was this lousy gold bathtub faucet."

**I^o Snoring**

## TEDDY HUSSEIN
tj@alpine.UUCP (T.J. Higgins)

*chuckle*

Have you heard that Teddy Kennedy is running for office in Baghdad?
Since all the bridges are gone, he should be a shoo-in.

## CHEMICAL WARFARE
scannell@bubba.ma30.bull.com (P Scannell)

*original, iraq, chuckle*

An executive of a German chemical company accused of selling raw
materials for chemical weapons to Iraq explained, *"We were only filling
orders."*

© 1991 Patrick D. Scannell. Used with Permission.

## ZERO TOLERANCE

crew@neon.stanford.edu (Roger Crew)

topical, sick, chuckle, iraq

A good caption for one of those pictures of the aftermath of the Iraqi flight from Kuwait — you know the scene: Kuwaiti freeways through the desert littered with bombed and abandoned vehicles everywhere, wreckage and bodies strewn all over the place:

SPEED LAWS ENFORCED
BY AIRCRAFT

## BILL CLINTON

apratt@atari.UUCP (Allan Pratt)

topical, chuckle

Well, Bill Clinton finally admitted that he'd tried pot, but he didn't inhale. I guess next we'll learn that he did date Gennifer Flowers after all, but he didn't come.

**:-j Left smiling smiley**

## DAYLIGHT SAVINGS TIME

bhayes@cs.stanford.edu (Barry Hayes)

topical, smirk

Anyone know how I can get my VCR to start blinking "1:00" now that Daylight Savings Time is here?

**:-k Beats me, looks like something, though**

## ORIGINAL, FAIRLY TOPICAL, DOW IMPLANTS

LAFORCE@xenon.arc.nasa.gov (Soren)

smirk, original

With all the attention that the Dow breast implants have been getting lately, I wondered why no one else has been manufacturing these "devices" except Dow.

Then I realized that everyone else was probably afraid of a "look and feel" lawsuit . . .

## MORE LA RIOTS

geoff@desint.UUCP (Geoff Kuenning)                    topical, heard it, chuckle

According to my friend Dave Bozman, they've brought additional charges against the men accused of beating truck driver Reginald Denny.

They are accused of impersonating police officers.

## U.S. CONSTITUTION 101

ipg@dcs.warwick.ac.uk (Ian Gent)
University of Warwick                                  original, topical, smirk

Two questions. Their relationship is for you to determine. One answer is given.

1. Who chooses the Vice President of the United States?

(Answer: The President.)

2. There is one person in the U.S. to whom the V.P.'s performance as President cannot possibly matter in any way. Name him.

:-: Mutant smiley

## BILL CLINTON

baldwin@csservera (LT J.D. Baldwin)                    topical, chuckle

From the "National Review":

They say the women in Arkansas are so fast, you have to put a governor on them.

## TYSON SENTENCE

andys@ulysses.att.com (Andy Sherman)
AT&T Bell Laboratories/Murray Hill, NJ                 topical, funny

Told by Larry Josephson in the closing credits of his public radio show "Modern Times."

Q. Why did they send Mike Tyson to prison?

A. *There were no more vacancies on the Supreme Court.*

## ROSS PEROT DEALS WITH THE PUBIC
larrabee@cse.ucsc.edu (Tracy Larrabee)                                 topical, funny

A friend from Texas reports:

This morning (June 11) I was watching a morning news program wherein a fluffy blonde (quite possibly Joan London) was tossing beach-ball type questions to Ross Perot. They opened up the lines for television audience questions, and the first caller (a seemingly normal-sounding taxpayer) posed the following two part question:

I have two questions, the first is as an outsider not affiliated with either party, how effective do you feel you will be in dealing with a partisan congress? And the second is, have you ever done a mind-meld with Howard Stern's penis?

Joan London, looking like the she had just bitten into a quince, turned to Ross Perot and said:

Well, perhaps you can answer the first part.

## JOKES FROM REAGAN'S SPEECH: THOMAS JEFFERSON
toma@romulus.cray.com (Thomas Arneberg)                                topical, funny

Reagan speech 8/17/92, referring to Bill Clinton (with veiled reference to Lloyd Bentson's comment to Dan Quayle during the 1988 VP debate; also after joking about his (Reagan's) advanced age):

All right. Listen to me. This fellow they've nominated claims he's the new Thomas Jefferson. Well, let me tell you something. I knew Thomas Jefferson. He was a friend of mine. And, governor, you're no Thomas Jefferson.

> **\*<:-) User is wearing a Santa Claus hat**

## SANTA'S UNMENTIONABLES
WKEOWN@ducvax.auburn.edu                                               topical, smirk

Here's one making the rounds:

Q. Why does Santa wear red underwear?

A. He's a man—he did all his laundry in one load.

## NEW VIDEO GAME: PACKMAN

bob@reed.edu (Robert Ankeney)                                topical, topical, original, funny

New from Ninnuendo — the PackMan (tm) game cartridge! Based on a familiar arcade game, this game finds the head of Senator Bob Packwood greedily munching bags of PAC money while being chased by a band of liberals. Upon munching the magic bottle of booze, the liberals turn into woman secretaries. See Bob chase them around desks! Bonus points on catching them. But beware of level 20, where they turn on him! On level 21, the liberals turn into members of the Ethics Committee! Though they may be even easier to evade, the booze bottles no longer work.

You'll have hours of fun being as evasive as Bob Packwood. Excellent for the would-be Congressman.

**:-\ Undecided smiley**

## SICK CHELSEA

greg@gallifrey.ucs.uoknor.edu (Greg Trotter)
Norman, Oklahoma                                              topical, chuckle

A relative heard this on C-Span the night of President Clinton's economic address...

Chelsea wasn't feeling well at her private school. She went to the infirmary to get some aspirin. The nurse discovered that nobody had ever signed a parental consent form to authorize the school to dispense medicine to the First Kid.

The nurse told Chelsea that they needed to contact one of her parents for permission to give her aspirin. Chelsea told her, *"Oh, please call Daddy. Mom's far too busy."*

## WOODY ALLEN'S GIRLS...

john@wpi.wpi.edu (John Stoffel)                               topical, chuckle

Heard this from folk singer Christine Lavin at her concert in Amherst, MA.

Did you hear that Woody Allen's girlfriend is pregnant with his next girlfriend?

### BOSNIA PEACE CONFERENCE
gnb@bby.com.au (Gregory Bond)                                    topical, chuckle

The Bosnian peace talks continued in Geneva today. The only thing that Alija Izetbegovic, Radovan Karadzic and Slobodan Milosovic could agree on was that John Major has a funny name.

### IT FIGURES
griffith@fx.com (Jim Griffith)                                   topical, chuckle

Larry Bud Melman is now the intellectual property of NBC.

### TOURISM, FLORIDA AND SICK HUMOR
j1h9453@eagle.tamu.edu (Joel Andrew Huddleston)              topical, chuckle, original

Given recent events in Florida, the tourism board in Texas has developed a new advertising campaign based on the slogan *"Ya'll come to Texas, where we ain't shot a tourist in a car since November 1963."*

### NIXON IS NO MORE..
tomhead@netcom.com (Tom Head)                                    topical, chuckle

This is original, but I'm sure others have come up with it as well:

Richard Milhous Nixon, former President of the United States, is dead. Let us now observe 18 and a half minutes of silence...

### MISPELLERS [SIC] OF THE WORLD, UNITE!
daugher@cs.tamu.edu (Walter Daugherity)
Texas A&M University                                            topical, true, chuckle

In an effort to snag more long distance telephone calls (charged to a credit card or a third number), AT&T reserved the toll-free number 1-800-OPERATOR. Not to be outdone, and perhaps knowing the public better, MCI reserved the number 1-800-OPERATER and has been scooping up calls intended for its arch-rival.

---

`C=:-) User is a chef`

# Chapter Four
# Later Internet Comedy

These are general jokes from **rec.humor.funny**'s early years which didn't fit in the other special categories (computers, topical jokes and true news). Also, a special item—the light bulb joke collection— is found at the end of this chapter.

---

### IRELAND FOREVER
peter@syacus.acus.oz.au (Peter Bell)
Australian Centre for Unisys Software, Sydney

heard it, chuckle

(This is an Irish joke with a twist. Told to me by my father-in-law.)

There is this American tourist on a trip around Ireland.

When the tour arrives at Belfast he decides to go for a stroll with the aim of taking in this new culture. After he's been walking for a while someone rushes up behind him and sticks a gun in his back.

The person says to the tourist, *"What are you, Catholic or Protestant?"*

The American thinks to himself *"Great— if I say I'm Catholic, this guy is sure to be Protestant. If I say I'm Protestant, he's sure to be Catholic. Either way I'm dead."* Then he has a brain wave and says to the guy, *"actually I'm Jewish."* This, he thinks to himself, will surely keep him safe.

The guy behind him then replies *"Gee, I must be the luckiest Arab in Ireland."*

---

## UP A CREEK

GARYE@MAX.ACS.WASHINGTON.EDU (Gary Ericson)                     funny, smirk

A biology graduate student went to Borneo to take some samples for his thesis work. He flew there, found a guide with a canoe to take him up the river to the remote site he where he would make his collections. About noon on the second day of travel up the river they began to hear drums. Being a city boy by nature, the biologist was disturbed by this. He asked the guide, *"What are those drums?"* The guide turned to him and said, *"Drums OK, but VERY BAD when they stop."*

Well the biologist settled down a little at this, and things went reasonably well for about two weeks. Then, just as they were packing up the camp to leave, the drums suddenly stopped! This hit the biologist like a ton of bricks (to coin a phrase), and he yelled at the guide,

*"The Drums have stopped, What happens now?"*

The guide crouched down, covered his head with his hands and said: *"Bass Solo."*

## PHONE A LOAN

2014_5001@uwovax.uwo.ca (Alexander R. Pruss)
Applied Math, U. of Western Ontario                     sexual, funny

A man approaches his best friend's wife one day when her husband is at the office. *"Will you have sex with me?"* he asks.

*"No. My husband wouldn't approve."*

*"O.K. What if I give you $1000?"*

*"Well, for $1000 I think I will. Come back tomorrow afternoon when my husband is at work."*

So the man shows up next day and slaps $1000 on the table and they do whatever it was they did(!) In the evening her husband comes home a little distraught: *"Was my best friend here today?"*

*"Y-y-yes."* his wife says with concern.

*"And did he leave $1000?"*

*"Y-y-yes."* she says expecting the worst.

*"Oh good, what a great pal he is. He came in this morning and asked if he could borrow $1000 from me and promised to return it this afternoon!"*

## EVERYTHING LOOKS BETTER WITH A FRESH COAT OF PAINT...

horsch@cs.ubc.ca (Michael Horsch)
Dept. of Computer Science, University of British Columbia heard it, funny

An eager, but less than bright, young entrepreneur decides to go into the painting business. So he wanders into the rich part of town, paint brush in hand, and knocks at the door of a large house.

*"Good day, sir. I was wondering if you had any painting you need done."*

The owner of the house, a rich man by any standard, looks speculatively at the painter. He perceives a vibrant entrepreneurial spirit, which reminds him of his own ambition in his younger days.

*"Hmmm. Yes, I think my porch needs a coat or two of paint."*

The eager young painter rushes off around the side of the house...

Several hours later, he returns to the front door, his clothes dripping paint, and knocks again.

*"Sir, I've finished! But I have to tell you, that wasn't a porch, it was a Ferarri."*

## NUN

pkuhio@uhccux.uhcc.hawaii.edu (Morton Cotlar) funny

A nun was sitting at a window in her convent one day... when she was handed a letter from home. Upon opening it a $10 bill dropped out. She was most pleased at receiving the gift from her home folks, but as she read the letter her attention was distracted by the actions of a shabbily dressed stranger who was leaning against a post in front of the convent.

She couldn't get him off her mind and, thinking that he might be in financial difficulties, she took the $10 bill and wrapped it in a piece of paper, on which she had written, "Don't despair, Sister Eulalia," and threw it out of the window to him. He picked it up, read it, looked at her with a puzzled expression, tipped his hat and went off down the street.

The next day she was in her cell saying her beads when she was told that some man was at her door who insisted on seeing her. She went down and found the shabbily dressed stranger waiting for her. Without saying a word he handed her a roll of bills. When she asked what they were for he replied, *"That's the sixty bucks you have coming. Don't Despair paid 5-1."*

## MORE THAN A MILE FOR THAT CAMEL

cs161fcz%sdcc10@ucsd.edu (cs161fcz) laugh, sexual

A nun and a priest were traveling across the desert and realized halfway across that the camel they were using for transportation was about to die. They set up a make-shift camp, hoping someone would come to their rescue, but to no avail. Soon the camel died.

After several days of not being rescued, they agreed that they were not going to be rescued. They prayed a lot (of course), and they discussed their predicament in great depth.

Finally the priest said to the nun, *"You know, Sister, I am about to die, and there's always been one thing I've wanted here on earth— to see a woman naked. Would you mind taking off your clothes so I can look at you?"*

The nun thought about his request for several seconds and then agreed to take off her clothes. As she was doing so, she remarked, *"Well, Father, now that I think about it, I've never seen a man naked, either. Would you mind taking off your clothes, too?"*

With little hesitation, the priest also stripped. Suddenly the nun exclaimed, *"Father! What is that little thing hanging between your legs?"*

The priest patiently answered, *"That, my child, is a gift from God. If I put it in you, it creates a new life."*

*"Well,"* responded the nun, *"forget about me. Stick it in the camel!"*

## STATUES COME TO LIFE

dg@lakart.UUCP (David Goodenough) sexual, scatological, smirk

One day, Cinderella's fairy godmother gets a bit drunk, and grants a wish to two statues in the park. Of course, they want to be brought to life for a while, so she does that, but says it's only for an hour. The two statues, a man and a woman, immediately head off into the bushes.

After only 30 minutes of much moaning and groaning, the couple returns.

*"You've still got 30 minutes left,"* says the fairy. *"Why not go back and enjoy some more?"*

*"OK,"* says the man. *"This time, it's my turn. You hold the pigeon down, and I'll sh\*t on its head."*

## HEAVEN AND HELL
egil@tc.fluke.COM (Kevin Summers)                                    funny

Heaven is a place where:

    The lovers are Italian
    The cooks are French
    The mechanics are German
    The police are English
    The government is run by the Swiss


Hell is a place where:

    The lovers are Swiss
    The cooks are English
    The mechanics are French
    The police are German
    The government is run by the Italians

---

**:v) Left -pointing nose smiley**

---

## NO COVER CHARGE
steven@uts.amdahl.com (Fearless Leader)                         sexual, funny

An elderly couple go to a physician complaining of non-specific sexual dysfunction, and ask the doctor if he will watch them having sex to determine if anything is wrong. After their romantic session, the MD assures them that everything seems fine and sends them on their way. One week later, they are back with the same complaint, and perform under his judgemental eye once more. Again, everything seems perfectly normal and he tells them so. Again, in one week's time, they appear and have sex while he watches. The MD, confused, tells them *"Look, this is the third time you've been in here, and NOTHING is wrong with the way you make love! What's really going on here?"*

*"Well,"* the elderly gentleman replies, *"you see, we're both married, but not to each other. So I can't go to her place, and she can't go to my place. Now Howard Johnson's charges $45 for a room, but you charge $35 for an office visit, plus we can write off 30% of this to Medicare."*

## MOSES AND JESUS PLAY GOLF

mikes@hpsrmjs.UUCP (Mike Seibel)                                    chuckle

One day Moses and Jesus were playing golf. They were at the tee of a beautiful par 3, with a lake right in the middle of the fairway. Moses selects a 5 iron, tees-up his ball and swings. His ball sails very high and lands in the middle of the lake. He mutters to himself and tees-up a second ball, this time selecting a 4 iron. This shot was perfect; landing right in the middle of the green.

Jesus pauses for a moment to ponder his club selection. *"Hmmmm..... Arnold Palmer would use this,"* he says as he picks up a 5 iron.

*"But, Jesus. My 5 iron shot ended up in the lake. You should use a 4 iron!"*

*"Nope. Arnie would use a 5,"* insisted Jesus.

So, Jesus swings hard and alas his shot ends up in the middle of the lake too. Jesus strolls over to the lake and walks out on the water to retrieve his ball. As Jesus is walking on the water trying to locate his ball a foursome comes up to the tee, sees a man walking on the water and one of them exclaims, *"Who does he think he is? Jesus Christ?"*

*"No,"* explains Moses, *"He is Jesus Christ. He thinks he's Arnold Palmer."*

## BIOLOGY IN AN IRISH HIGH SCHOOL

dwv@ihuxz.UUCP (Dave Vollman)                                    sexual, chuckle

Mr. Flanagan was teaching his biology class, and quizzing them on last nights reading assignment.

*"Shannon, can you tell me which organ in the human body can expand to several times its normal size?"* asked Mr. Flanagan

Shannon giggled as if she were thinking of something unmentionable in class.

*"Sean, can you tell me?"* asked Mr. Flanagan.

*"The Eye,"* said Sean.

*"That's right,"* and Mr. Flanagan continued, *"Shannon, I'll tell you three things that are for sure."*

*"First, you did not do your reading last night and that's for sure."*

*"Second, you have a very dirty mind, and that's for sure."*

*"And Third, you are going to be DAMN disappointed, and THAT'S FOR SURE."*

## WHAT'S THE DIFFERENCE?
clark@watmath.UUCP (Steve Clark)
National Institute for Standards and Technology

sexual, funny

It seems that a little girl and and a little boy are arguing about differences between the sexes, he arguing that boys are inherently better and she that girls are. The subject, of course, spills over into the personal realm, so that the real issue is which of the two children is superior. Finally, the boy drops his pants and says, *"Here's something I have that you'll never have!"*

The little girl is pretty upset by this, since it is quite clearly true. She turns and runs home.

A while later, she comes running back with a smile on her face. She drops *her* pants, and says, *"My mommy says that with one of these, I can have as many of those as I want!"*

---

**:-b Left-pointing tongue smiley**

---

## GOD AND THE POST OFFICE
TheMessenger@cit5.cit.oz.au (TheMessenger)
Chisholm Institute of Technology, Melbourne, Australia

heard it, chuckle

A nice young worker from Australia Post (yes they do exist), was sorting through her regular envelopes, when she discovered a letter addressed as follows:

> GOD
> c/o Heaven

Upon opening the envelope, a letter enclosed told of how a little old lady who had never asked for anything in her life, was desperately in need of $100 and was wondering if God could send her the money.

Well the young lady was deeply touched and made a collection from her fellow workmates and collected $90 and sent it off to the old lady. A few weeks later another letter arrived addressed to God, so the young lady opened it and it read *"Thank you for the money, God, I deeply appreciate it, however I only received $90. It must have been those bastards at the Post Office."*

## THE PICKLE SLICER!

t_longst@colby.UUCP (Thomas _. Longstaff)    heard it, chuckle, sexual

Bill worked in a pickle factory. He had been employed there for a number of years when he came home one day to confess to his wife that he had a terrible compulsion. He had an urge to stick his penis in the pickle slicer. His wife suggested that he should see a therapist to talk about it, but Bill indicated that he'd be too embarrassed. He vowed to overcome the compulsion on his own.

One day a few weeks later Bill came home absolutely ashen. His wife could see at once that something was seriously wrong. *"What's wrong, Bill?"* she asked.

*"Do you remember that I told you how I had this tremendous urge to put my penis in the pickle slicer?"*

*"Oh, Bill, you didn't."*

*"Yes, I did."*

*"My God, Bill, what happened?"*

*"I got fired."*

*"No, Bill. I mean, what happened with the pickle slicer?"*

*"Oh... she got fired too."*

**:-/ Lefty undecided smiley**

## BIRDS AND THE BEES

applic@philmtl.philips.ca (Papyrus Development)    sexual, funny, rec.humor_cull

There is this French couple, sitting up talking, when the wife says to the husband that it was time he had a conversation with their thirteen year old son about the birds and the bees.

So the father goes to his son's room and says, *"Son, do you remember that session I arranged for you with mademoiselle Ginette?"*

*"Oh yes papa, I remember very well,"* says the son.

*"Well son, it is time you knew that the birds and the bees do the same thing."*

## TAKE A LETTER, MARIA...

peghiny@milpnd.enet.dec.com (Bluegrass For Breakfast)                    heard it, funny

MEMORANDUM

From: Headquarters - New York
To: General Managers

Next Thursday at 10:30 Halley's Comet will appear over this area. This is an event which occurs only once every 75 years. Notify all directors and have them arrange for all employees to assemble on the Company lawn and inform them of the occurrence of this phenomenon. If it rains, cancel the day's observation and assemble in the auditorium to see a film about the comet.

MEMORANDUM

From: General Manager
To: Managers

By order of the Executive Vice President, next Thursday at 10:30, Halley's Comet will appear over the Company lawn. If it rains, cancel the day's work and report to the auditorium with all employees where we will show films: a phenomenal event which occurs every 75 years.

MEMORANDUM

From: Manager
To: All Department Chiefs

By order of the phenomenal Vice President, at 10:30 next Thursday, Halley's Comet will appear in the auditorium. In case of rain over the Company lawn, the Executive Vice President will give another order, something which occurs only every 75 years.

MEMORANDUM

From: Department Chief
To: Section Chiefs

Next Thursday at 10:30 the Executive Vice President will appear in the auditorium with Halley's Comet, something which occurs every 75 years. If it rains, the Executive Vice President will cancel the comet and order us all out to our phenomenal Company lawn.

MEMORANDUM

From: Section Chief
To: All EA's

When it rains next Thursday at 10:30 over the Company lawn, the phenomenal 75 year old Executive Vice President will cancel all work and appear before all employees in the auditorium accompanied by Bill Halley and his Comets.

[Ed: There are many variants of this.]

---

**:-? Smiley smoking a pipe**

---

## WELCOME TO THE CHURCH

rhunt@med.unc.edu

heard it, funny, sexual

Three married couples, aged 20, 30, and 40 years old, want to join the Orthodox Church of Sexual Repression. Near the end of the interview, the priest informs them that before they can be accepted they will have to pass one small test. They will have to abstain from all sex for a month. They all agree to try.

A month later they are having their final interview with the cleric. He asks the 40 year old couple how they did. *"Well, it wasn't too hard. I spent a lot of time in the workshop and she has a garden so we had plenty of other things to do. We did OK."* the husband said.

*"Very good, my children. You are welcome in the Church. And how well did you manage?"* he asked the 30 year old couple.

*"It was pretty difficult,"* the husband answered. *"We thought about it all the time. We had to sleep in different beds and we prayed a lot. But we were celibate for the entire month."*

*"Very good, my children. You are welcome in the Church. And how about you?"* he asked the 20 year old couple.

*"Not too good, I'm afraid, Father. We did OK for the first week.,"* he said sheepishly. *"By the second week we were going crazy with lust. Then one day during the third week my wife dropped a head of lettuce, and when she bent over to pick it up, I... I weakened and took her right there."*

*"I'm sorry my son, you are not welcome in the Church"*

*"Yeah, and we're not too welcome in the A&P anymore, either."*

## "SHIT HAPPENS" IN VARIOUS RELIGIONS

stuart@orac.hq.ileaf.com (Stuart Freedman x1708)          swearing, offense=religious, chuckle

First set from: pszila@u.washington.edu (Peter Szilard) and kamens@neon.stanford.edu (Samuel N. Kamens)

TAOISM:  Shit happens.

CONFUCIANISM:  Confucious says, "Shit happens."

BUDDHISM:  If shit happens, it isn't really shit.

HINDUISM:  This shit has happened before.

PROTESTANTISM:  If shit happens, it happens to someone else.

CATHOLICISM:  If shit happens, you deserved it.

JUDAISM:  Why does shit always happen to US?

ISLAM:  If shit happens, kill the person(s) responsible.

More-From: sunne!East!bruces (Bruce Sesnovich - Sun BOS Information Architecture)

EXISTENTIALISM:  Shit doesn't happen; shit is.

JEHOVAH'S WITNESSES:  No shit happens until Armaggedon.

ISLAM:  When shit happens, kill Salman Rushdie.

SECULAR HUMANISM:  Shit evolves.

REFORM JUDAISM:  Got any Kaopectate?

CHRISTIAN SCIENCE:  When shit doesn't happen, don't call a doctor—pray.

## SCHOLARLY SHIT HAPPENS

poy@fiuggi.irvine.dg.com (David Poyourow)          swearing, scatological, original, chuckle

I sent the "Shit Happens in Various Religions" to my friend John Stark, who happens to have a PhD in Religious Studies. A week later he sent me his revised version, which is pretty serious, but also pretty funny.

TAOISM: Shit Happens, so flow with it.

CONFUCIANISM: Confucius says, "If shit has to happen, let it happen *properly*.

BUDDHISM: If shit happens, it isn't really happening *to* anyone.

HINDUISM: This shit happening *is* you.

PROTESTANTISM: If shit happens, praise the Lord for it!

JUDAISM: Why does shit always happen just before closing the deal?

ISLAM: Shit happening is Allah's Will.

EXISTENTIALISM: Shit happening is absurd!

ZEN: What is the sound of shit happening?

## BLACK HUMOUR

mas@castle.edinburgh.ac.uk (M Smith)

Edinburgh Concurrent Supercomputer Project                          swearing, funny

*I got this one from my Uncle over the Christmas Holidays, I've no idea where he got it from....*

A seven year-old turns up in his classroom one morning to be confronted by his teacher:

Teacher: *Morning Tommy, and why weren't you at school yesterday?*

Tommy: *Well Miss, my Grandad got burnt.*

Teacher: *Oh Dear, he wasn't too badly hurt I hope?*

Tommy: *Oh yes Miss, they don't fuck around at those crematoriums.*

## GENEALOGY

GEO.DOSCH@genie.com                                                   chuckle

From "Dear Abby" newspaper column:

**Dear Abby:** I have always wanted to have my family history traced, but I can't afford to spend a lot of money to do it. Any suggestions?
— *Sam in California*

**Dear Sam:** Yes. Run for public office.

**,-} Wry and winking**

## MALE BIRTH CONTROL

SPELL@kuhub.cc.ukans.edu                              sexual stereotypes, sexual, funny

(I heard this on a Kansas City radio station.)

Did you know that they just invented a male birth control pill?

*You take one the next morning and it changes your blood type.*

## THE DAY OF THE WEDDING

spillman%emily.uvm-gen.uvm.edu (spillman william b)          sexual, funny, offence=monarchists

I heard this from a Welsh friend of mine, Peter Gardiner, who lives in London.

It is the wedding day of Prince Charles and Lady Di. Charles had been up late the night before boozing with his old Navy buddies, woke up late, threw on his clothes and rushed to the Royal Coach and set off. In the coach, he noticed that he had forgotten his shoes, so he borrowed the ones his valet was wearing, but they were 2 sizes too small.

Charles made it through the ceremony, then through the reception with his feet in agony the whole time, and finally with great relief, went upstairs with his new bride.

Their departure was noticed by the Queen and Queen Mother who followed them up and listened at the the door. First they heard, *"Ohhh, ohhh, that feels so goood, it was sooo tight."*

*"I told you she was,"* said the Queen to the Queen Mother.

Then they heard, *"Ohhh, ohhh, ohhh, ahhhh, that feels even better, and it was a lot tighter."*

*"Tsk tsk tsk,"* said the Queen Mother, *"Once a sailor, always a sailor."*

**.-] One-eyed smiley**

## ADAM AND EVE

gar@spiff.cminc.com (Gordon Runkle)          heard it, funny, sexual stereotypes

This is from Reader's Digest ("Laughter, the Best Medicine"),

*"I'm lonely,"* Adam told God in the Garden of Eden. *"I need to have someone around for company."*

*"Okay,"* replied God. *"I'm going to give you the perfect woman. Beautiful, intelligent and gracious— she'll cook and clean for you and never say a cross word."*

*"Sounds good,"* Adam said. *"But what's she going to cost?"*

*"An arm and a leg."*

*"That's pretty steep,"* countered Adam. *"What can I get for just a rib?"*

## BREAST FIXATION

jmh%coyote.UUCP@cs.arizona.edu (John Hughes) — sexual, funny

One day this fellow noticed that a new couple had moved into the house next door. He was also quick to notice that the woman liked to sunbathe in the backyard, usually in a skimpy bikini that showed off a magnificent pair of breasts. He made it a point to water and trim his lawn as much as possible, hoping for yet another look. Finally, he could stand it no more. Walking to the front door of the new neighbor's house, he knocked and waited. The husband, a large, burly man, opened the door.

*"Excuse me,"* our man stammered, *"but I couldn't help noticing how beautiful your wife is."*

*"Yeah? So?"* his hulking neighbor replied.

*"Well, in particular, I am really struck by how beautiful her breasts are. I would gladly pay you ten thousand dollars if I could kiss those breasts."*

The burly gorilla is about to deck our poor guy when his wife appears and stops him. She pulls him inside and they discuss the offer for a few moments. Finally, they return and ask our friend to step inside.

*"OK,"* the husband says gruffly, *"for ten thousand dollars you can kiss my wife's tits."*

At this the wife unbuttons her blouse, and the twin objects of desire hang free at last. Our man takes one in each hand, and proceeds to rub his face against them in total ecstasy. This goes on for several minutes, until the husband gets annoyed. *"Well, come on already, kiss 'em!"* he growls.

*"I can't,"* replies our awe-struck hero, still nuzzling away.

*"Why not?"* demands the husband, getting really angry now.

*"I don't have ten thousand dollars."*

## MEDICAL MARVELS

crm@cs.duke.edu (Charlie Martin) — sexual stereotypes, funny

This is making the rounds here. . .

Duke University Medical Center is reporting an unusual occurrence in the Obstetrics department: a child was born with both male and female organs.

A penis and a brain.

## GOOD NEWS AND BAD NEWS
sater@cs.vu.nl (Hans van Staveren)                    heard it, funny

A man gets a telephone call from a doctor. The doctor says: "About this medical test I did on you, I have some good news and some bad news."

The man asks for the good news first:

*"The good news is that you have 24 hours to live,"* says the doctor.

The man, incredulously: *"If that is the good news, then what is the bad news??"*

*"I couldn't reach you on the phone yesterday."*

## BOTTOM UP PLANNING
mitchb@frith.egr.msu.edu (Bradley A Mitchell)            heard it, smirk, scatological

In the beginning was the Plan
And then came the Assumptions
And the Assumptions were without form
And the Plan was completely without substance
And the Darkness was on the faces of the Employees

And they spoke unto their Supervisors saying
*"It's a Crock of Shit and it Stinketh!"*

And the Supervisors went unto their Department Heads and sayeth
*"It's a Pail of Dung, and none may abide the Odor thereof."*

And the Department Heads went unto their Managers, and sayeth unto them
*"It is a Container of Excrement, and it is very strong, such that none may abide by it."*

And the Managers went unto their Director and sayeth
*"It is a Vessel of Fertilizer, and none may abide its Strength."*

And the Director went unto the Vice President and sayeth
*"It contains that which aids Plant Growth, and it is very Strong."*

And the Vice President went to the Executive Vice President and sayeth
*"It promoteth Growth, and it is very Powerful."*

And the Executive Vice President went to the President and sayeth
*"This Powerful New Plan will actively promote the Growth and Efficiency of the System."*

And the President looked upon the Plan and saw that it was Good
And the Plan became Policy.

## A LITTLE 69
BM.H2H@rlg.UUCP (Philip Miller, Dr.)                                          funny, sexual

A Chinese couple is in bed one night, when the man gives his wife an elbow and says, "May-Ling, how about a little 69. I'm in the mood for some 69."

*"Shut-up and go back to sleep,"* groans his wife.

*"Come on, you know I like 69, and for that matter, so do you!"*

*"What time is it?"*

*"1:30."*

*"You want me to get up at this hour and make beef and broccoli for the two of us?"*

[Attributed to Rabbi Boruch Lipsky and reportedly also in Playboy]

**O-) Smiley cyclops (scuba diver?)**

## LAWYER'S AGE
milun@cs.buffalo.edu (Davin Milun)                                          funny

Joe the lawyer died suddenly, at the age of 45. He got to the gates of Heaven, and the angel standing there said, *"We've been waiting a long time for you."*

*"What do you mean,"* he replied, *"I'm only 45, in the prime of my life. Why did I have to die now?"*

*"45? You're not 45, you're 82,"* replied the angel.

*"Wait a minute. If you think I'm 82 then you have the wrong guy. I'm only 45. I can show you my birth certificate."*

*"Hold on. Let me go check,"* said the angel and disappeared inside. After a few minutes the angel returned. *"Sorry, but by our records you are 82. I checked all the hours you have billed your clients, and you have to be 82 . . ."*

## NAME CHANGES

sfleming@cs.heriot-watt.ac.uk

funny

A recent questionnaire sent out in the Soviet Union contained the questions:

1. Where were you born?
2. Where did you go to school?
3. Where did you attain your majority?
4. Where do you wish to live?

One return provided the following answers:

1. St. Petersburg
2. Petrograd
3. Leningrad
4. St. Petersburg

## WACKY WHIRLY BIRDS

adeboer@gjetor.geac.com (Anthony DeBoer)
GEAC Systems, Toronto

funny

I heard this from my brother, who is a Search and Rescue pilot at Canadian Forces Base Bagotville, Quebec. It's an apocryphal story that allegedly happened late one night during bad weather, as heard over the tower radio:

Helicopter Pilot: *"Roger, I'm holding at 3000 over <such-and-such> beacon."*

Second voice: *"NO! You can't be doing that! I'm holding at 3000 over that beacon!"*

(brief pause, then first voice again): *"You idiot, you're my co-pilot."*

## DALAI LAMA IN NYC

jonb@ingres.com (Jon Berger)

chuckle

The Dalai Lama walks up to a hot dog vendor and says, *"Make me one with everything."*

## THE THREE MONKS

ray@biovision.toronto.edu (Ray Deonandan)                    scatological, funny, offense=religious

There were three pious monks. These monks were so pious, in fact, that the head abbot decided one day to reward their devotion by granting them each one day of sin, on the condition that they confess their activities to him at the end of the day.

So, the day cometh, and the three monks go off into the night to indulge in all manner of sin.

The first monk saunters in at 1:00 in the morning, and tries to sneak upstairs to bed. But the head abbot, who was waiting up for the three, stopped him and demanded that he relate his doings.

"No, head abbot," the first monk said, "it's too evil for me to admit!"

"The deal was for you to tell me everything you did, otherwise you will not receive absolution!" said the abbot.

So the first monk agreed to tell what he did. "I - I - I drank! And I did all manner of drugs! And I smoked tea bags and old polyester ties, and I snorted coffee whitener...."

"Enough!" said the head abbot, enraged. "Those are evil sins, but I promised to forgive you. Go out back, drink some Holy Water, say some prayers and you will be forgiven in the morning."

The first monk thankfully went off to follow the abbot's instructions.

The second monk wanders in at 2:00 AM. "What did you do last night?" demanded the head abbot.

"I can't say! It's much too evil!"

"The agreement was that you must tell me everything you did!"

"Okay," agreed the second monk. "I had all manner of sex. I had sex with young girls, young boys, small furry quadrupeds, large species of flora, my CD player..."

"Enough!" cried the head abbot. "That is a truly great sin. But I promised to give you absolution. Go out back and drink some Holy Water. Then say some prayers and you will be forgiven in the morning."

The second monk sauntered off to do just that.

And the third and final monk crawls in at 3:00 in the morning.

"What," asks the head abbot, "did you do this evening?"

"No, head abbot, it's too great a sin to admit. I cannot tell!"

*"The agreement, monk! You must tell me!"*

The third monk bowed his head and nodded. *"All right, head abbot. Last night I . . . I . . ."*

*"Yes?"*

*"I pissed in the Holy Water."*

---

## THE FIRST CLEAN SHEEP JOKE I EVER HEARD
USERSUPY@ualtamts.bitnet (Allen George Supynuk)                    funny

Substitute <ethnic origin> below for the place of origin of any ethnic group not locally renowned for high intelligence.

A man walks up to a New Zealand sheep farmer and says, *"If I can tell you exactly how many sheep you have down there, can I keep one?"*

The farmer glances at the vast array of sheep, snickers, and says, *"Sure."*

The man looks carefully at the sheep, then says, *"5,279."*

The farmer, startled, says, *"How did you do that?"*

The man says, *"I'd rather not say. Can I have my animal?"*

*"I guess so,"* says the farmer. The man picks up an animal and starts to walk away.

*"Wait!"* yells the farmer. *"If I can guess where you're from, will you give me my animal back?"*

The man snickers, and says, *"Sure."*

*"You're from <ethnic origin>,"* says the farmer.

The man, startled, says, *"How did you do that?"*

The farmer says, *"I'd rather not say. Can I have my dog back?"*

---

## DIPLOMACY
sfleming@cs.heriot-watt.ac.uk                    funny

[The following, possibly apocryphal, story appeared in the Glasgow Herald.]

Lord George Brown, when the band struck up at an embassy function, asked: *"Beautiful lady in scarlet, will you waltz with me?"*

*"Certainly not,"* was the reply. *"First, you are drunk. Second, it is not a waltz, but the Venezuelan national anthem; and third, I am not a beautiful lady in scarlet, but the papal nuncio."*

---

## CHOICE OF RELIGION
S.PERUZZI@genie.com (Sherry)                                  funny, religious stereotypes

This was told to me recently by a Unitarian divinity student, who said she heard it from an Episcopalian divinity student, so it must be okay!

A Jew, a Catholic and an Episcopalian were standing at the gates of Hell. Satan came out, and looked them over.

*"Why are you here?"* he asked the Jew. *"I ate pork,"* the Jew admitted. *"Okay, come on in,"* replied Satan. Then he turned to the Catholic.

*"What are you doing here?"* Satan asked the Catholic. *"I ate meat on Friday long before His Holiness said it was okay,"* the Catholic answered. *"Well, then, come in,"* Satan said.

Then he looked at the Episcopalian. *"Why on earth are you down here?"* Satan asked. The Episcopalian hung his head in shame as he answered:

*"I used the wrong fork."*

## SEEN IN REC.GAMES.BRIDGE
msb@sq.com (Mark Brader)                                                  funny

Q: What is the worst possible bridge hand you can have?

*A: 4 aces, 4 kings, 4 queens, and 2 jacks.*

## LAWYER JOKES
BEER.MUG@genie.com (Marc)                                                 funny

After successfully passing the bar exam, a man opened his own law office. He was sitting idle at his desk when his secretary announced that a Mr. Jones had arrived to see him. *"Show him right in!"* our lawyer replied. As Mr. Jones was being ushered in our lawyer had an idea. He quickly picks up the phone and shouts into it " *...and you tell them that we won't accept less then fifty thousand dollars, and don't even call me until you agree to that amount!"* Slamming the phone down he stood up and greeted Mr. Jones; *"Good Morning, Mr. Jones, what can I do for you?"*

*"I'm from the phone company,"* Mr. Jones replied, *"I'm here to connect your phone."*

## ANYBODY HOME?

patrickm@sco.com (Patrick K. Moffitt)
Santa Cruz Operation

*funny*

I heard this from my uncle John Herbert. You can't offend anyone with it.

A telephone sales person makes a call to an unknown prospect and a very small, very soft, very quiet, and obviously young person answers the phone.

Sales person: *Hello, may I speak to the man of the house please?*

Youngster: (whispering) *No, he's busy.*

Sales person: *Well then, can I please speak to your mother?*

Youngster: (in a whisper) *She's busy too.*

Sales person: *I see, how about your brother? Can I speak to him?*

Youngster: (whispering) *No. He's busy too.*

Sales person: (losing patience) *Is your sister there? Can I talk to her?*

Youngster: (in a whisper) *She's busy too.*

Sales person: ( by now quite exasperated) *What are all these people doing that keeps them so busy?!!!*

Youngster: (still whispering) *Looking for me.*

---

:-=) Older smiley with mustache

---

## "NO SOLICITORS"— WE MEAN IT

friedl@mtndew.tustin.ca.us (Stephen J. Friedl)

*chuckle*

[ believed to be original from my officemate Scott Wallace ]

We get hit up by door-to-door salespeople all the time, and they always seem to miss the "Absolutely no solicitors" sign on the door. My officemate put up a new sign:

TO SOLICITORS:
Please remove rings, watches, belt buckles, and other metal objects before entering. Our pit bull has trouble digesting such items. Thank you for your cooperation.

## HI-TECH HAIKUS

damon@sunburn.stanford.edu (Damon A. Koronakos)                    original, chuckle

Brian Roberts and I wrote these in a moment (hour?) of boredom.

one with nintendo
halcyon symbiosis
hand thinks for itself

oh no godzilla
guns and planes cannot stop him
tokyo is ablaze

cold matsushita
their technology stronger
enslaves our people

samurai fighter
keyboard and mouse are his sword
digital battles

midori ito
girl finds glory, is broken
they can rebuild her

DAT arrives
frequency notch treachery
people are not fooled

honda seatcovers
winter warm and summer cool
little lambs no more

young Sony worker
innocent hands build Walkman
tears run down faces

the sand remembers
once there was beach and sunshine
but chip is warm too

**:u) Smiley with funny-looking left nose**

## THE JOKE THAT MADE RHF INFAMOUS

brian@radio.uucp (Brian Glendenning)
Radio Astronomy, University of Toronto                    racist (mildly), chuckle

(Relayed From prabhu@mitisft)
[Ed: This is it! The big joke that got rec.humor.funny splattered on the front pages of major newspapers and banned at the University of Waterloo and Stanford!]

A Scotsman and a Jew went to a restaurant. After a hearty meal, the waitress came by with the inevitable check. To the amazement of all, the Scotsman was heard to say, *"I'll pay it!"* and he actually did.

The next morning's newspaper carried the news item:

"JEWISH VENTRILOQUIST FOUND MURDERED IN BLIND ALLEY."

## TO ERR IS HITLER

Bear's_Class_Account@ub.cc.umich.edu                                         funny

The following began life as a Top Ten list of "Mistakes Made by Adolf Hitler." it was passed around during a lecture in a political science class of mine and soon grew to over 100 entries. I have culled out the stupid and/or truly offensive ones, as well as any that said nasty things about any particular nationality (read, the French.) You'll have to excuse the fact that some of them are rather obscure, but that's what happens when you get a bunch of political scientists in the same room. Without further ado, I give you...

## Top 50 Mistakes Made by Adolf Hitler

1. Land War in Asia
2. Changed name from highly catchy "Schickelgruber" to boring "Hitler"
3. Leaving his little mustache: not growing a friendly Abe Lincoln beard to instill trust among subjects
4. Not buying lifts for his shoes
5. Failure to exploit Me 262 Messerschmidt
6. Failure to exploit Eva Braun
7. Chose swastika as party symbol rather than the daisy
8. Chose Josef Goebels rather than Marlene Dietrich to promote Nazi image
9. Chose "Deutschland Uber Alles" over "Let's All Be There" as party slogan
10. Lost the Ark to Indiana Jones
11. Chose unfashionable blacks and browns rather than trendy plaids and stripes as uniform colors for SS & SA
12. Referring to Stalin as "that old Georgian fat back"
13. Indiscriminate use of V-2 rockets for public fireworks displays
14. Free beer in munitions plants
15. Lisp never corrected
16. Bad toupee
17. Refused to undergo nostril reduction surgery
18. Failed to conquer strategically important Comoros Islands
19. Fell asleep in staff meetings
20. Chose Italy as ally
21. Got involved with a Sicilian when death was on the line
22. Made pass at Eleanor Roosevelt during 1936 Olympics

23. Built heliport on top of new Reichstag building which looked remarkably like a bullseye from the air

24. Always got Churchill out of bed for conference calls

25. Never had fireside mass rallies

26. Told Einstein he had a stupid name

27. Used SS instead of LAPD

28. Admired Napoleon's strategy

29. Strong fondness for sauerkraut and beans made General Staff avoid him constantly

30. In last days, chose to hide in bunker rather than ask U.S. for a little country place in Hawaii

31. Nightmare involving Pillsbury Doughboy haunted him constantly with war advice

32. Major theme in speeches — *lebensraum*, or "living room" — widely misperceived as call for domestic architectural reform

33. Failed to revoke Rudolph Hess' pilot licence

34. Pissed off Jesse Owens at 1936 Olympics

35. Didn't put his brother Billy in the concentration camps. When word got out that Billy was just a beer guzzling fat guy in a small town in Bavaria who grew peanuts it was bad P.R. for Der Fuhrer

36. Breast feeding for too long

37. Passed up Finnish "tanks for snowshoes" offer before invasion of USSR

38. Drank too much at Beer Hall Putsch

39. Spent jail time planning how to conquer the world instead of his own escape

40. Forgot to write "Dear Joey" letter to Stalin before invasion of Poland

41. Blew nose on Operation Barbarossa maps, forcing extemporaneous invasion of Soviet Union

42. Took no steps to keep Neville Chamberlain in power

43. Chose the Tirpitz for that weekend of love with Eva in the fjords

44. Frequently mistaken for Charlie Chaplin due to mustache; undermined credibility (as when he threatened to invade Poland, everyone waited for the punchline)

45. Came off as poor loser when "Triumph of the Will" failed to win Oscar for "Best Foreign Documentary" — "You don't like me" speech undermined image

46. Used to make prank calls to FDR asking if he had "Prince Albert in a can"

47. Forgot correct interpretation of Nietzsche; caused much embarrassment when he used to cite philosophical support for his concept of the "Oberdude"

48. Got drunk on schnapps and suggested Tojo attack the U.S. saying, "The U.S. only has twenty times your industrial power, what are you, a wimp?"

49. Listened to too much Wagner and not enough Peter, Paul and Mary

50. Spent too much on screwdrivers and toilet seats

---

## RADAR TRAP
mikes@hpsrmjs.sr.hp.com (Mike Seibel)                                    chuckle

From Herb Caen's column in the San Francisco Chronicle:

A motorist was unknowingly caught in an automated speed trap that measured his speed using radar and photo his car. He later received in the mail a ticket for $40, and a photo of his car. Instead of payment, he sent the police department a photograph of $40. Several days later, he received a letter from the police department that contained another picture— of handcuffs.

---

**:-' Smiley spitting out its chewing tobacco**

---

## HUSBAND AND WIFE
rog@ingres.com (Roger Taranto)                                           funny

Because the husband had just gotten home from a six-month tour of duty, the husband and wife were furiously making love when, all of a sudden, the wind slammed a door shut somewhere else in the house.

The husband says, *"Oh no! That must be your husband coming home."*

And the wife replies, *"No. He's off in the Navy for six months."*

---

## 20 THINGS THAT NEVER HAPPEN IN "STAR TREK"

nick@lfcs.edinburgh.ac.uk (Nick Rothwell)                    funny

(Article from Edinburgh University's MIDWEEK Student Magazine, by Graeme MacDonald.)

1. The Enterprise runs into a mysterious energy field of a type it has encountered several times before.

2. The Enterprise goes to visit a remote outpost of scientists, who are all perfectly all right.

3. Some of the crew visit the holodeck, and it works properly.

4. The crew of the Enterprise discover a totally new lifeform, which later turns out to be a rather well-known old lifeform wearing a funny hat.

5. The crew of the Enterprise are struck by a mysterious plague, for which the only cure can be found in the well-stocked Enterprise sick-bay.

6. The Captain has to make a difficult decision about a less advanced people which is made a great deal easier by the Starfleet Prime Directive.

7. The Enterprise successfully ferries an alien VIP from one place to another without serious incident.

8. An enigmatic being composed of pure energy attempts to interface to the Enterprise's computer, only to find out that it has forgotten to bring the right leads.

9. A power surge on the Bridge is rapidly and correctly diagnosed as a faulty capacitor by the highly-trained and competent engineering staff.

10. The Enterprise is captured by a vastly superior alien intelligence which does not put them on trial.

11. The Enterprise is captured by a vastly inferior alien intelligence which they easily pacify by offering it some sweeties.

12. The Enterprise visits an earth-type planet called "Paradise" where everyone is happy all of the time. However, everything is soon revealed to be exactly what it seems.

13. A major Starfleet emergency breaks out near the Enterprise, but fortunately some other ships in the area are able to deal with it to everyone's satisfaction.

14. The Enterprise is involved in a bizarre time-warp experience which is in some way unconnected with the Late 20th Century.

15. Kirk (or Riker) falls in love with a woman on a planet he visits, and isn't tragically separated from her at the end of the episode.

16. Counsellor Troi states something other than the blindingly obvious.

17. The warp engines start playing up a bit, but seem to sort themselves out after a while without any intervention from boy genius Wesley Crusher.

18. Wesley Crusher gets beaten up by his classmates for being a smarmy git, and consequently has a go at making some friends of his own age for a change.

19. Spock (or Data) is fired from his high-ranking position for not being able to understand the most basic nuances of about one in three sentences that anyone says to him.

20. Most things that are new or in some way unexpected.

*But we still love it, right kids?*

---

## RABBI UP TO THE BAR, BOYS

L.GRAHAM4@genie.com (Lori)                                          funny

A Rabbi walks into a bar to use the restroom. He walks up to the bartender, and asks *"Can I please use the restroom?"* The place was hoppin' with music, and dancin', till they saw the Rabbi. The bartender says, *"I really don't think you should."*

The Rabbi again, asks, *"Can I please use the restroom?"* Well, the bartender says to the Rabbi, *"I really don't think you should, you see, there is a statue of a beautiful naked lady, and she's only covered by a fig leaf!"*

The Rabbi responded with, *"Nonsense a man of my stature will not be bothered by that statue!"* Well, the bartender showed the Rabbi the door at the top of the stairs.

The Rabbi proceeded to the restroom, and after a few minutes, he came back out, and the whole place was hoppin' with music and dancin' again! He went to the bartender and said, *"Sir, I don't understand, when I came in here, the place was hoppin' with music and dancin', then the place became absolutely quiet. I went to the restroom, and the place is hoppin' again."*

The bartender says, *"Well, now you're one of us, can I get you a drink?"* The Rabbi says, *"I still don't understand."* The bartender told him, *"You see, everytime the fig leaf is lifted on the statue, the lights go out in the whole place. Now, can I get you a drink?"*

---

**:-} Beard**

---

## NATURAL CHILDBIRTH

sue@ariel.ucs.unimelb.edu.au (Sue McPherson)
Software Contracts Group, University of Melbourne, Australia

chuckle

This sounds a lot like an urban myth, but my brother-in-law tells me that this happened to the wife of someone he works with. I must admit that I'm a bit sceptical but its certainly worth a chuckle.

It seems that this lady didn't quite make it to hospital for the birth of her child, in fact, the baby was born on the lawn just outside the main entrance. The poor woman was dreadfully embarrassed and was being consoled by one of the Nurses, who said; *"Don't worry about it. It could have been worse, why two years ago we had a woman who gave birth in the elevator."* The woman cried *"That was me!"* and burst into tears.

## COSTUME PARTY

bscott@isis.cs.du.edu (Ben Scott)

heard it, sexual, funny

Sam and Susan were invited to a costume party. Susan went out and rented costumes for the both of them. However, when the time came for the party, Susan wasn't feeling well and Sam went on alone.

A few hours later, Susan began to feel better and decided to go on to the party. She realized that while she knew Sam was in a gorilla suit, he had never seen her costume, and decided to go and see what he got up to while he was alone.

She arrived and observed him dancing closely with a series of beautiful women. She approached him and began flirting, and soon they were taking a walk in the woods alone. They then undressed in the darkness and had sex.

She got home before her husband and when he arrived, she was in bed. She asked him, *"How was the party?"*

He replied *"Oh, the usual - you know I never have much fun at these things alone."*

*"Didn't you even dance?"* she asked.

*"No, I sat in the den all night playing cards. The guy I lent my costume to had a ball, though..."*

:> **Midget smiley**

## WHY GO TO MED SCHOOL?

well!alcmist (Frederick Wamsley)                                    heard it, chuckle

<from Richard Buchmiller>

A pipe burst in a doctor's house. He called a plumber. The plumber arrived, unpacked his tools, did mysterious plumber-type things for a while, and handed the doctor a bill for $600.

The doctor exclaimed, *"This is ridiculous! I don't even make that much as a doctor!"* The plumber waited for him to finish and quietly said, *"Neither did I when I was a doctor."*

## WAIT'LL NEXT YEAR...

phssra@unix.cc.emory.edu (Scott R. Anderson)                               laugh

From a local BBS:

During Operation Desert Storm, Gen. Schwartzkopf was walking about in the Kuwaiti desert, and stumbled across something in the sand. Uncovering it, he found an old lamp. He took the lamp back to his tent and proceeded to polish it up, and (of course) out pops a Genie.

The Genie thanked Schwartzkopf for releasing him from imprisonment, and told him that he would grant him any wish that he desired. The General thought a moment and then unrolled a map of the Middle East onto his table. He explained to the Genie about the wars that had been ravaging the entire area, and his one wish was for peace throughout the region. The Genie responded that he and his ancestors had been working on that problem for several thousand years, had had no success, and now consider it hopeless. He asked the General if there was another wish he could grant instead.

Schwartzkopf thought for a moment and finally said that he wished that the Chicago Cubs could finally win a World Series. The Genie pondered a moment and then said, *"Why don't we take another look at that map?"*

**:< Midget unsmiley**

## LIGHT BULB JOKES

kurt@tc.fluke.COM (Kurt Guntheroth)          offensive to hundreds of stereotypes, funny

[Ed: Mr. Guntheroth has collected these jokes together from various sources, and has given permission for their inclusion in this book. He reserves other collector's rights. Two of the jokes in here are mine!]

Here it is...the canonical collection. Note that I don't attribute these jokes, and I have made editorial changes in some. The collection is canonical in that I try to keep only one of each " kind" of joke, and avoid jokes like " Q: How many FOO...? A: Something about FOO that has nothing whatsoever to do with light bulbs." I also delete jokes so topical or obscure they could never be understood except in deep context.

Updated May 24, 1988

Accept no substitutes; this is the original and only complete Canonical Collection of Light Bulb Jokes, from the original author.

It is possible to construct infinite small variations by substituting particular ethnic groups into these jokes, or by expanding certain jokes into seventy line monsters. I have resisted this impulse.

Of course you may substitute any ethnic group for <ethnic>. I feel it would be inappropriate for me to pick on a single ethnic group when there are so many and when I don't know your personal prejudices.

The WASPs in the following jokes are 'White Anglo-Saxon Protestants' and are assumed to represent any upper-middle class, loose-lifestyle people. In Seattle, these are 'Mercer Islander' jokes. In California, they are 'Marin County' jokes, and so on. Some of these jokes are also told as 'Jewish American Princess' jokes.

WARNING: This file contains material of a satirical nature. It may be offensive to members of the following groups:

| | | | |
|---|---|---|---|
| Californians | Oregonians | New Yorkers | Jersey-ans |
| Politicians | Communists | Pro-lifers | Feminists |
| Parents | Babies | Students | Frat rats |
| Economists | Soldiers | WASPs | Animals |
| Athletes | Artists | Professors | Psychiatrists |
| Doctors | Lawyers | Accountants | Managers |
| Christians | Jews | Buddhists | Gods |
| Polish people | Russians | <Ethnics> | Homosexuals |
| Hardware people | Tech Writers | Marketing people | Software people |
| Necrophiliacs | FSEs | | |

and by now many others who are no doubt offended to have been left off this list.

# THE CANONICAL COLLECTION OF LIGHT BULB JOKES

Q: How many Californians does it take to change a light bulb?
A: *Six. One to turn the bulb, one for support, and four to relate to the experience.*

Q: How many Oregonians does it take to screw in a light bulb?
A: *Five. One to change the bulb and four more to chase off the Californians who have come up to relate to the experience.*
A': *Nine. One to change the bulb, and eight to protest the nuclear power plant that generates the electricity that powers it.*

Q: How many New Yorkers does it take to screw in a light bulb?
A: *None 'o yo' fuckin' business!*
A'': *50. 50? Yeah 50; it's in the contract.*

Q: How many WASPs does it take to change a light bulb?
A: *Two. One to call the electrician and one to mix the martinis.*

Q: How many Psychiatrists does it take to change a light bulb?
A: *Only one, but the bulb has got to really WANT to change.*
A': *None; the bulb will change itself when it is ready.*

Q: How many software people does it take to screw in a light bulb?
A: *None. That's a hardware problem.*
A': *One, but if he changes it, the whole building will probably fall down.*
A'': *Two. One always leaves in the middle of the project.*

Q: How many hardware folks does it take to change a light bulb?
A: *None. That's a software problem.*
A': *None. They just have marketing portray the dead bulb as a feature.*

Q: How many FSE's does it take to replace a dead light bulb?
A: *Who can tell. FSE's are always in the dark.*
A': *2. One to hold the bulb and one to pound it in (etc)*
Note: FSE's are " Field Service Engineers."

Q': How long will it take?
A': *That's indeterminate. It depends on how many dead bulbs they've brought with them.*

Q": What if you have two dead bulbs?
A": *They replace your fuse box.*

Q: How many Unix hacks does it take to change a light bulb?
A: *As many as you want; they're all virtual, anyway.*

Q: How many APL hackers does it take to screw in a light bulb?
A: *None. There's a primitive for that.*

Q: How many Bell Labs Vice Presidents does it take to change a light bulb?
A: *That's proprietary information. Answer available from AT&T on payment of license fee (binary only).*
A': *Nearly unanswerable, since the one who tries to change it usually drops it, and the others call for a planning session.*
A": *Three. One to get the bulb and two to get the phone number of one of their subordinates to actually change it.*

Q: How many graduate students does it take to screw in a light bulb?
A: *Only one, but it may take upwards of five years for him to get it done.*

Q: How many 'Real Men' does it take to change a light bulb?
A: *None: 'Real Men' aren't afraid of the dark.*
A': *None of your damn business!*

Q: How many 'Real Women' does it take to change a light bulb?
A: *None: A 'Real Woman' would have plenty of real men around to do it.*

Q: How many Jewish mothers does it take to screw in a light bulb?
A: *None. (" That's all right...I'll just sit here in the dark...")*

Q: How many mice does it take to screw in a light bulb?
A: *Only two, but the hard part is getting them into the light bulb.*

Q: How many WASPs does it take to screw in a light bulb?
A: *Silly, WASPs don't screw in a light bulb, they screw in a hot tub.*

Q: How many Marxists does it take to screw in a light bulb?
A: *None: The light bulb contains the seeds of its own revolution.*

Q: How many (Generals/Politicians) does it take to change a light bulb?
A: *1,000,001: One to change the bulb and 1,000,000 to rebuild civilization to the point where they need light bulbs again.*

Q: How many Russian leaders does it take to change a light bulb?
A: *Nobody knows. Russian leaders don't last as long as light bulbs.*

Q: How many nuclear engineers does it take to change a light bulb?
A: *Seven. One to install the new bulb and six to figure out what to do with the old one for the next 10,000 years.*

Q: How many pre-med students does it take to change a light bulb?
A: *Five: One to change the bulb and four to pull the ladder out from under him.*

Q: How many Christians does it take to change a light bulb?
A: *Three, but they're really only one.*

Q: How many Christian Scientists does it take to screw in a light bulb?
A: *None, but it takes at least one to sit and pray for the old one to go back on.*

Q: How many Roman Catholics does it take to screw in a light bulb?
A: *Two. One to do the screwing, and one to hear the confession.*

Q: How many jugglers does it take to change a light bulb?
A: *One, but it takes at least three light bulbs.*

Q: How many Feminists does it take to change a light bulb?
A: *That's not funny!!!*

Q: How many supply-siders does it take to change a light bulb?
A: *None. The darkness will cause the light bulb to change by itself.*

Q: How many economists does it take to screw in a light bulb?
A: *Two. One to assume the ladder and one to change the bulb.*
A': *None. If the government would just leave it alone, it would screw itself in.*

Q: How many Valley Girls does it take to change a light bulb?
A: *Oooh, like, manual labor? Gag me with a spoon! For sure.*

Q: How many data base people does it take to change a light bulb?
A: *Three: One to write the light bulb removal program, one to write the light bulb insertion program, and one to act as a light bulb administrator to make sure nobody else tries to change the light bulb at the same time.*

Q: How many straight San Franciscans does it take to screw in a light bulb?
A: *Both of them.*

Q: How many Zen masters does it take to screw in a light bulb?
A: *A tree in a golden forest.*
A′: *Two: one to change the bulb and one not to change it.*
A″: *One to change and one not to change is fake Zen. The true Zen answer is Four. One to change the bulb.*
A‴: *None. Zen masters carry their own light.*

Q: How many Carl Sagans does it take to screw in a light bulb?
A: *Billions and billions.*

Q: How many folk singers does it take to screw in a light bulb?
A: *Two. One to change the bulb, and one to write a song about how good the old light bulb was.*

Q: How many surrealists does it take to change a light bulb?
A: *Two, one to hold the giraffe, and the other to fill the bathtub with brightly colored machine tools.*

Q: How many gorillas does it take to screw in a light bulb?
A: *Only one, but it sure takes a shitload of light bulbs!*

Q: How many doctors does it take to screw in a light bulb?
A: *Three. One to find a bulb specialist, one to find a bulb installation specialist, and one to bill it all to Medicare.*

Q: What is the difference between a pregnant woman and a light bulb?
A: *You can unscrew a light bulb.*

Q: How many [IBM] Technical Writers does it take to change a light bulb?
A: *100. Ten to do it, and 90 to write document number GC7500439-0001, Multitasking Incandescent Source System Facility, of which 10% of the pages state only, " This page intentionally left blank," and 20% of the definitions are of the form " A <. . .> consists of sequences of non-blank characters separated by blanks."*

A′: *Just one, provided there's an engineer around to explain.*

Q: How many Bratzlaver Chassidim does it take to change a light bulb?
A: *None. They will never find one that burned as brightly as the first one.*

Q: How many gays does it take to screw in a light bulb?
A: *Two. One to screw it in and the other to say " Fabulous."*

Q: How many professors does it take to change a light bulb?
A: *Only one, but they get three tech. reports out of it.*

Q: How many people from New Jersey does it take to change a light bulb?
A: *Three. One to change the light bulb, one to be a witness, and the third to shoot the witness.*

Q: How many <ethnics> does it take to screw in a light bulb?
A: *10. One to hold the bulb and nine to rotate the ladder.*

Q: How many strong <ethnics> does it take to screw in a light bulb?
A: *115. One to hold the bulb and 114 to rotate the house.*

Q: How many <ethnic> gods does it take to screw in a light bulb?
A: *Two. One to hold the bulb and the other to rotate the planet.*

Q: How many cops does it take to screw in a light bulb?
A: *None. It turned itself in.*

Q: How many lawyers does it take to change a light bulb?
A: *How many can you afford?*
A': *It only takes one to change your bulb...to his.*
A'': *Lawyers don't change bulbs. Now if you're looking for someone to really screw a bulb...*

Q: How many football players does it take to change a light bulb?
A: *The entire team! And they all get a semester's credit for it!*

Q: How many Lesbians does it take to screw in a light bulb?
A: *Three. One to screw it in and two to talk about how much better it is than with a man.*

Q: How many Federal employees does it take to screw in a light bulb?
A: *Sorry, that item has been cut from the budget!*

Q: How many psychics does it take to screw in a light bulb?
A: —— *You should have hit "n!"*

Q: How many "pro-lifers" does it take to change a light bulb?
A: *6: 2 to screw in the bulb and 4 to testify that it was lit from the moment they began screwing.*

Q: How many sorority sisters does it take to change a light bulb?
A: *51. One to change the bulb, and fifty to sing about the bulb being changed.*

Q: How many frat guys does it take to screw in a light bulb?
A: *Three: One to screw it in, and the other two to help him down off the keg.*
A': *Five: One to hold the bulb, and four to guzzle beer until the room spins.*
A'': *None. Frat boys screw in puddles of vomit.*

Q: How many Harvard grads does it take to screw in a light bulb?
A: *Just one. He grabs the bulb and waits for the world to revolve around him.*

Q: How many bureaucrats does it take to screw in a light bulb?
A: *Two. One to assure the everything possible is being done while the other screws the bulb into the water faucet.*
A': *45. One to change the bulb, and 44 to do the paperwork.*

Q: How many board meetings does it take to get a light bulb changed?
A: *This topic was resumed from last week's discussion, but is incomplete pending resolution of some action items. It will be continued next week. Meanwhile...*

Q: How many assholes does it take to change a light bulb?
A: *None; assholes never see the light anyway.*

Q: How many Necrophiliacs does it take to screw in a light bulb?
A: *None. Necrophiliacs prefer dead bulbs.*
A': *Only one. " Oh, excuse me, could you please test the socket with your finger while I go get a new bulb?"*

Q: How many brewers does it take to change a light bulb?
A: *About one third less than for a regular bulb.*

Q: How many WASP Princesses does it take to screw in a light bulb?
A: *Two. One to get a Tab and one to call Daddy.*

Q: How many accountants does it take to screw in a light bulb?
A: *What kind of answer did you have in mind?*

Q: How many junkies does it take to screw in a light bulb?
A: *"Oh wow, is it like dark, man?"*

Q: How many consultants does it take to change a light bulb?
A: *I'll have an estimate for you a week from Monday.*

Q: How many U.S marines does it take to screw in a light bulb?
A: *50. One to screw in the light bulb and the remaining 49 to guard him.*

Q: How many Romulans does it take to screw in a light bulb?
A: *151, one to screw the light-bulb in, and 150 to self-destruct the ship out of disgrace. (Warning: do not tell this to Romulans or be ready for a fight. They consider this joke to be a disgrace, though it is not bad for a LBJ.)*

Q: How many editors of Poor Richard's Almanac does it take to replace a light bulb?
A: *Many hands make light work.*

Q: How many Vulcans does it take to change a light bulb?
A: *Approximately 1.0000000000000000000000000*

Q: How many efficiency experts does it take to replace a light bulb?
A: *None. Efficiency experts replace only dark bulbs.*

Q: How many Pygmies does it take to screw in a light bulb?
A: *At least three. (Notes: think height!)*

Q: How many actors does it take to change a light bulb?
A: *Only one. They don't like to share the spotlight.*

Q: How many Chinese Red Guards does it take to screw in a light bulb?
A: *10,000 - to give the bulb a cultural revolution.*

Q: How many anarchists does it take to screw in a light bulb?
A: *All of them.*

Q: Do you know how many musicians it takes to change a light bulb?
A: *No, big daddy, but hum a few bars and I'll fake it.*
A': *Twenty. One to hold the bulb, two to turn the ladder, and seventeen in on the guest list.*

Q: How many mystery writers does it take to screw in a light bulb?
A: *Two, one to screw it almost all the way in and the other to give it a surprising twist at the end.*

Q: How many bikers does it take to change a light bulb?
A: *It takes two. One to change the bulb, and the other to kick the switch.*

Q: How many Taoists does it take to change a light bulb?
A: *You cannot change a light bulb. By its nature it will go out again.*

Q: How many running-dog lackeys of the bourgeoisie does it take to change a light bulb?
A: *Two. One to exploit the proletariat, and one to control the means of production!*

Q: How many referral agents does it take to screw in a light bulb?
A: *Two: One to screw you out of a fee, and the other to send you to a store where they ran out of bulbs weeks ago.*

Q: How many existentialists does it take to screw in a light bulb?
A: *Two: One to screw it in and one to observe how the light bulb itself symbolizes a single incandescent beacon of subjective reality in a netherworld of endless absurdity reaching out toward a maudlin cosmos of nothingness.*

Q: How many dull people does it take to change a light bulb?
A: *one.*

Q: How many big black monoliths does it take to change a light bulb?
A: *Sorry, light bulbs are an evolutionary dead end.*

Q: How many light bulbs does it take to change a light bulb?
A: *One, if it knows its own Goedel number.*

Q: How many dadaists does it take to screw in a light bulb?
A: *To get to the other side.*

Q: How many mathematicians does it take to screw in a light bulb?
A: *None. It's left to the reader as an exercise.*
A': *One. He gives it to six Californians, thereby reducing the problem to an earlier joke.*
A'': *One. He gives it to five Oregonians, thereby reducing the problem to an earlier joke.*
A''': *In an earlier article, zeus!bobr writes:*

> Q: How many mathematicians does it take to screw in a light bulb?
> A: *One. He gives it to six Californians, thereby reducing the problem to an earlier joke...*
>
> *In earlier work, Wiener [1] has shown that one mathematician can change a light bulb.*
>
> *If k mathematicians can change a light bulb, and if one more simply watches them do it, then k+1 mathematicians will have changed the light bulb.*
>
> *Therefore, by induction, for all n in the positive integers, n mathematicians can change a light bulb.*
>
> Bibliography: [1] Wiener, Matthew P., <11485@ucbvax, Re: YALBJ, 1986

Q: How many consultants does it take to change a light bulb?
A: *We don't know. They never get past the feasibility study.*

Q: How many Ukrainians does it take to screw in a light bulb?
A: *None, because people who glow in the dark don't need light bulbs.*
Note: Topical to the Chernobyl Reactor disaster of 1984.

Q: How many poets does it take to change a light bulb?
A: *Three. One to curse the darkness, one to light a candle... and one to change the bulb.*

Q: How many stock brokers does it take to change a light bulb?
A: *Two. One to take out the bulb and drop it, and the other to try and sell it before it crashes (knowing that it's already burned out).*
A': *It's out?? Sell my G.E. stock NOW!*

Q: How many magicians does it take to change a light bulb?
A: *Depends on what you want to change it into.*

Q: How many missionaries does it take to change a light bulb?
A: *101. One to change it and 100 to convince everyone else to change light bulbs too.*

Q: How many Teamsters does it take to change a light bulb?
A: *"Twelve. Ya got a problem with that?"*

Q: How many surgeons does it take to replace a light bulb?
A: *3. We'd also like to remove the socket as you aren't using it now.*

Q: How many conservatives does it take to change a light bulb?
A: *One; after reflecting in the twilight on the merit of the previous bulb.*

Q: How many libertarians does it take to change a light bulb?
A: *Libertarians never change light bulbs, because someone might enter the room who wants to sit in the dark.*

Q: How many Macintosh users does it take to change a light bulb?
A: *None. You have to replace the whole motherboard.*

Q: How many nihilists does it take to change a light bulb?
A: *There is nothing to change.*

Q: How many televangelists does it take to screw in a light bulb?
A: *None. Televangelists screw in motels.*

Q: How many presidential candidates does it take to change a light bulb?
A: *Fewer and fewer all the time.*

Q: How many believable, competent, " just-right-for-the-job" presidential candidates does it take to change a light bulb?
A: *It's going to be a dark 4 years, isn't it?*

---

## POLITICAL SCIENCE LESSON
ken@richp1.UUCP (Ken Marks)
Rich Inc., Chicago

heard it, funny

It's time for some political nonsense (redundant?)

### A LESSON IN POLITICAL SCIENCE

**SOCIALISM** — You have two cows. The government takes one to give to someone else.

**COMMUNISM** — You have two cows. The government takes both and gives you the milk.

**FASCISM** — You have two cows. The government takes both and sells you the milk.

**NAZISM** — You have two cows. The government takes both and shoots you.

**BUREAUCRACY** — You have two cows. The government takes both, shoots one and pours the milk down the drain.

**CAPITALISM** — You have two cows. You sell one and buy a bull.

**ANARCHY** — Steal neighbour's bull, shoot the government.

---

## POPULAR EUROPEAN LANGUAGES
likeness@cs.ucsd.edu (Don Likeness)

original, smirk

Here is an original joke by Lewis W. Call, and myself.

A small survey of some popular European languages:

**Spanish**—Everything you say makes you sound hungry.
**Russian**—There are 33 differerent ways to say, "Comrade, pass the Vodka or I shoot you.
**French**—Every French sentence carries the implicit connotation that you want to have sex with the person you are talking to.
**German** —The German word for *"hello"* is *"Echsteinlefahrtengruber."* The German translation for *"Hey, Hans what say tomorrow morning we climb into our tanks and roll over Poland?"* is *"Hans, Poland, ja?"*

---

**O:-) User is an angel (at heart, at least)**

---

# Chapter Five
# True News

Because **rec.humor.funny** is user-contributed, it also attracts stories of funny real-life events experienced by or related to the participants. These stories are all true or supposedly true—this is known as "found humour" and is often some of the most entertaining comedy there is. I hope that all these rate a smile from you.

Also included here are some things that were intended to be funny or clever, but were simply reported by readers who witnessed them. Snappy comebacks, bumper stickers, T-shirts, etc. all belong here.

---

## DISORDER IN THE COURT

wlui@batcomputer.tn.cornell.edu (Wayne Lui)
Cornell Theory Center, Cornell University, Ithaca NY

funny

Disorder in the Court: a Collection of 'Transquips' collected by Richard Lederer, reprinted in N.H. Business Review

Most language is spoken language, and most words, once they are uttered, vanish forever into the air. But such is not the case with language spoken during courtroom trials, for there exists an army of courtroom reporters whose job it is to take down and preserve every statement made during the proceedings.

Mary Louise Gilman, the venerable editor of the National Shorthand Reporter has collected many of the more hilarious courtroom bloopers in two books - Humor in the Court (1977) and More Humor in the Court, published a few months ago. From Mrs. Gilman's two volumes, here are some of my favorite transquips, all recorded by America's keepers of the word:

Q. *What is your brother-in-law's name?*

A. *Borofkin.*

Q. *What's his first name?*

A. *I can't remember.*

Q. *He's been your brother-in-law for years, and you can't remember his first name?*

A. *No. I tell you I'm too excited.* (Rising from the witness chair and pointing to Mr. Borofkin.) *Nathan, for God's sake, tell them your first name!*

Q. *Did you ever stay all night with this man in New York?*

A. *I refuse to answer that question.*

Q. *Did you ever stay all night with this man in Chicago?*

A. *I refuse to answer that question.*

Q. *Did you ever stay all night with this man in Miami?*

A. *No.*

Q. *Now, Mrs. Johnson, how was your first marriage terminated?*

A. *By death.*

Q. *And by whose death was it terminated?*

Q. *Doctor, did you say he was shot in the woods?*

A. *No, I said he was shot in the lumbar region.*

Q. *What is your name?*

A. *Ernestine McDowell.*

Q. *And what is your marital status?*

A. *Fair.*

Q. *Are you married?*

A. *No, I'm divorced.*

Q. *And what did your husband do before you divorced him?*

A. *A lot of things I didn't know about.*

Q. *And who is this person you are speaking of?*

A. *My ex-widow said it.*

Q. *How did you happen to go to Dr. Cherney?*

A. *Well, a gal down the road had had several of her children by Dr. Cherney, and said he was really good.*

Q. *Do you know how far pregnant you are right now?*

A. *I will be three months November 8th.*

Q. *Apparently then, the date of conception was August 8th?*

A. *Yes.*

Q. *What were you and your husband doing at that time?*

Q. *Mrs. Smith, do you believe that you are emotionally unstable?*

A. *I should be.*

Q. *How many times have you committed suicide?*

A. *Four times.*

Q. *Doctor, how many autopsies have you performed on dead people?*

A. *All my autopsies have been performed on dead people.*

Q. *Were you acquainted with the defendant?*

A. *Yes, sir.*

Q. *Before or after he died?*

Q. *Officer, what led you to believe the defendant was under the influence?*

A. *Because he was argumentary and he couldn't pronunciate his words.*

Q. *What happened then?*

A. *He told me, he says, "I have to kill you because you can identify me."*

Q. *Did he kill you?*

A. *No.*

Q. *Mrs. Jones, is your appearance this morning pursuant to a deposition notice which I sent to your attorney?*

A. *No. This is how I dress when I go to work.*

THE COURT: *Now, as we begin, I must ask you to banish all present information and prejudice from your minds, if you have any.*

Q. *Did he pick the dog up by the ears?*

A. *No.*

Q. *What was he doing with the dog's ears?*

A. *Picking them up in the air.*

Q. *Where was the dog at this time?*

A. *Attached to the ears.*

Q. *When he went, had you gone and had she, if she wanted to and were able, for the time being excluding all the restraints on her not to go, gone also, would he have brought you, meaning you and she, with him to the station?*

MR. BROOKS: *Objection. That question should be taken out and shot.*

Before we recess, let's listen to one last exchange involving a child:

Q. *And lastly, Gary, all your responses must be oral. O.K.? What school do you go to?*

A. *Oral.*

Q. *How old are you?*

A. *Oral.*

---

**):-) Smiley big face**

---

## CALIFORNIA RAISINS

johne@hpvcljh.UUCP (john eaton)                                    true, chuckle

According to Harpers Index, sales of California Raisin™ merchandise in North America topped $450 million last year. Sales of actual California raisins were only $400 million during the same period.

---

***:o) And Bozo the Clown!**

---

## GURKHAS - THE MARTIAL RACE

dhesi@bsu-cs.UUCP (Rahul Dhesi)
Mukund Srinivasan Department of Civil Engineering, Johns Hopkins

true, chuckle

(From an article in soc.culture.indian:)

GURKHAS - THE MARTIAL RACE

Now that an accord has been signed between the GNLF of Subhash ( not the go back to India one :-)) Ghising and the Government of India, it might be appropriate to recollect an interesting anecdote regarding these doughty warriors.

In World War II, an English reporter who had heard so much about the bravery and elan of the Gurkhas visited a camp just in front of the enemy lines (Germans). During the course of his reporting, he had occasion to observe a mission being conducted.

The mission was to airdrop a bunch of soldiers behind enemy lines to conduct some relatively light action. He watched the commander of the Gurkhas (a British soldier) pitch the mission and then ask for volunteers. To his surprise, only about half the Gurkhas volunteered and were sent off.

Throughly disillusioned with the legends of Gurkha bravery, the reporter went back home. After the war, he happened to run into a Gurkha who had been there, and asked him why half the troops had failed to volunteer. It turned out that none of the squad, both those who volunteered and those who did not, were aware that they would get a parachute for the drop. Hence the low turnout.

## DOUBLE NEGATIVES

baulch@thiazi.cs.cornell.edu (Garth Baulch)
Cornell Univ. CS Dept, Ithaca NY

chuckle

A linguistics professor was lecturing to his class one day about the fact that in many languages, such as English, a double negative forms a positive, while in other languages, such as Russian, a double negative is still a negative. *"However,"* he pointed out, *"in no language can a double positive form a negative."*

A bored voice from the back of the room responded, *"Yeah, yeah...."*

## PRACTICAL JOKE DOWN SOUTH

djones@megatest.UUCP (Dave Jones)
Megatest Corporation, San Jose, CA

true, funny

I used to work for T.I. in Houston. Once a young programmer fellow from Bedford, England came to do some consulting. He was a nice enough guy, but very stiff and proper. On his last day before returning to G.B., I took him to lunch at a Luby's Cafeteria. While waiting in line, I told him that before he left Texas, he simply must try some mepyew.

He said, *"What?"*

I said, *"Mepyew. It is very popular. Everyone here eats it with lunch. Sort of a Texas tradition. The woman in the serving line will ask you if you want some."*

I give a sly wink or two to various prospective diners who were overhearing the conversation and looking quizzical.

He agreed to order some mepyew.

We approached the first station where the lady was selling jello deserts and chilled salads.

*"Mepyew?"* she asked.

*"Yes please,"* he responded.

*"Mepyew?"*

*"Yes."*

*"Mepyew?"* (Now with noticeable agitation.)

*"Yes! If you Please!"*

*"Well ahm not a mind reader!"*

I laughed a little.

Finally realizing that he had been had, he proceded directly to the roast beef and mashed potatoes, as any good Englishman would.

I giggled. The people I had winked at giggled. My English friend busied himself with macaroni and cake.

Back at the office, Sheila and Mike giggled. The Englishman studied a directory listing. Someday, I'm going to invent a dish called mepyew. Maybe it will be a jello and roast beef casserole.

## TIRED AND COMPLAINING

mosurm@mntgfx.UUCP (Mosur Mohan)

The following is an actual letter of complaint which I grabbed off the net many years ago (when it used to be called net.jokes, if you can remember that long ago!) Unfortunately, I don't have the original source anymore. Note the date sent and the prices quoted.

Atlanta, Georgia
September 13, 1970

Director
Billing Department
Shell Oil Company
P.O. Box XXXX
Tulsa, Oklahoma 74102

Dear Sir:

I have been a regular customer of the Shell Oil Company for several years now, and spend approximately $40.00 per month on Shell products. Until recently, I have been completely satisfied with the quality of Shell products and with the service of Shell employees.

Included in my most recent statement from your department was a bill for $12.00 for a tire which I purchased at the Lowell I. Reels Shell station in McAdenville, N.C. I stopped at this station for gasoline and to have a timing malfunction corrected. The gasoline cost $5.15; eight new plugs cost $9.36; labor on the points $2.50. All well and good.

Earlier in the day I had a flat tire, which the attendant at the Lowell I. Reels station informed me that he was unable to fix. He suggested that I purchase a tire from him in order that I have a spare for the remainder of my journey to Atlanta. I told him that I preferred to buy tires from home station in Atlanta, but he continued to stress the risk of driving without a spare. My reluctance to trade with an unknown dealer, even a Shell dealer, did not discourage him and finally, as I was leaving, he said that out of concern for my safety (my spare was not new) and because I had made a substantial expenditure at his station, he would make me a special deal. He produced a tire ("Hits a good one. Still has the tits on it. See them tits. Hits a twenty dollar tar.") which I purchased for twelve dollars and which he installed on the front left side for sixty-five cents. Fifty miles further down the highway, I had a blowout.

Not a puncture which brought a slow, flapping flat, nor a polite ladyfinger firecracker rubberburpple rupture (pop); but a howitzer blowout, which reared the the hood of my car up into my face, a blowout, sir, which tore a flap of rubber from this "tire" large enough to make soles for both sandals of a medium sized hippie. In a twinkling, then, I was driving down Interstate 85 at sixty miles per hour on three tires and one rim with rubber clinging to it in desperate shreds and patches, an instrument with a bent, revolving, steel-then-rubber-then-steel rim, whose sound can be approximated by the simultaneous placing of a handful of gravel and a young duck into a Waring Blender.

The word "careen" does no justice whatever to the movement that the car then performed. According to the highway patrolman's report, the driver in the adjoining lane, the left hand— who, incidentally, was attempting to pass me at the time— ejaculated adrenelin all over the ceiling of his car. My own passengers were fused into a featureless quiver in the key of "G" in the back seat of my car. The rim was bent; the tits were gone; and you can f—k yourself with a cream cheese dildo if you entertain for one moment the delusion that I intend to pay the twelve dollars.

Sincerely yours,

---

## VIDEO TROUBLE

michelsn@bimacs.cs.biu.ac.il (Akiva Michelson)          funny, true, iraq

Michael Covington writes:

Phone call actually received by someone I know, from next-door neighbor:

*"Our cable TV is having interference right now, is yours?"*

*"Not as far as I know... what channel are you watching?"*

*"We're not watching a channel. We're playing a tape."*

During the Gulf war, here in Israel, there was a family watching the Cosby show, and taping it just in case there would be another air-raid siren. Sure enough there was, and they filed into their sealed rooms. After the whole thing was over, they returned to watch their video tape. And what do you know, the same thing happened just about the same time in the show. After they retuned to their sealed room for a third time they realized it was the tape and not a real drill.

---

## THE COOLIDGE EFFECT

mjb@mentor.cc.purdue.edu (Matthew Bradburn)                    true, chuckle

a supposedly true story from:
Bermant, G. (1976). Sexual behavior: Hard times with the Coolidge Effect. In M. H. Siegel & H. P. Zeigler (Eds.), /Psychological Research: The inside story/ (pp. 76-103). New York: Harper & Row.

One day the President and Mrs. Coolidge were visiting a government farm. Soon after their arrival they were taken off on separate tours. When Mrs. Coolidge passed the chicken pens she paused to ask the man in charge if the rooster copulates more than once each day. *"Dozens of times,"* was the reply. *"Please tell that to the President,"* Mrs. Coolidge requested.

When the President passed the pens and was told about the roosters, he asked, *"Same hen every time?"* *"Oh no, Mr. President, a different one each time."* The President nodded slowly, then said, *"Tell that to Mrs. Coolidge."*

## AIRLINE JOKE

LUPES@csi.compuserve.com

chuckle

Eastern Airlines recently introduced a special half fare for wives who accompanied their husbands on business trips. Expecting valuable testimonials, the PR department sent out letters to all the wives of businessmen who had used the special rates, asking how they enjoyed their trip.

Letters are still pouring in asking, *"What trip?"*

## MORT SAHL ON HAIG

john@jupiter.nmt.edu (John Shipman)                    true, funny

I heard Mort Sahl tell this story about Al Haig on the CBS morning TV program; this version is paraphrased from my notes.

When Prime Minister Nakasone visited President Reagan, he asked for the auto import restrictions to be rescinded, saying *"We've had a rougher time of it; consider Hiroshima."*

The Gipper was nonplused. *"What has that got to do with it?"*

*"Well, we've never destroyed one of your cities,"* replied Nakasone.

Quickly Haig cut in: *"What about Detroit?"*

## SIGNS OF OUR TIMES
vixie@decwrl.dec.com (Paul A Vixie)                                    funny, true

[Ed: From a book called Anguished English, by Richard Lederer.  Reproduced with his permission, so long as you run out and buy his book!]

### Some do's and don't do's for all you travelers

IN A TOKYO HOTEL: Is forbitten to steal hotel towels please. If you are not person to do such thing is please not to read notis.

IN ANOTHER JAPANESE HOTEL ROOM: Please to bathe inside the tub.

In a Bucharest hotel lobby: The lift is being fixed for the next day. During that time we regret that you will be unbearable.

IN A LEIPZIG ELEVATOR: Do not enter the lift backwards, and only when lit up.

IN A BELGRADE HOTEL ELEVATOR: To move the cabin, push button for wishing floor. If the cabin should enter more persons, each one should press a number of wishing floor. Driving is then going alphabetically by national order.

IN A PARIS HOTEL ELEVATOR: Please leave your values at the front desk.

IN A HOTEL IN ATHENS: Visitors are expected to complain at the office between the hours of 9 and 11 A.M. daily.

IN A YUGOSLAVIAN HOTEL: The flattening of underwear with pleasure is the job of the chambermaid.

IN A JAPANESE HOTEL: You are invited to take advantage of the chambermaid.

IN THE LOBBY OF A MOSCOW HOTEL ACROSS FROM A RUSSIAN ORTHODOX MONASTERY: You are welcome to visit the cemetery where famous Russian and Soviet composers, artists, and writers are buried daily except Thursday.

IN AN AUSTRIAN HOTEL CATERING TO SKIERS: Not to perambulate the corridors in the hours of repose in the boots of ascension.

ON THE MENU OF A SWISS RESTAURANT: Our wines leave you nothing to hope for.

ON THE MENU OF A POLISH HOTEL: Salad a firm's own make; limpid red beet soup with cheesy dumplings in the form of a finger; roasted duck let loose; beef rashers beaten up in the country people's fashion.

IN A HONG KONG SUPERMARKET: For your convenience, we recommend courageous, efficient self-service.

OUTSIDE A HONG KONG TAILOR SHOP: Ladies may have a fit upstairs.

IN A BANGKOK DRY CLEANER'S: Drop your trousers here for best results.

OUTSIDE A PARIS DRESS SHOP: Dresses for street walking.

IN A RHODES TAILOR SHOP: Order your summers suit. Because is big rush we will execute customers in strict rotation.

SIMILARLY, FROM THE SOVIET WEEKLY: There will be a Moscow Exhibition of Arts by 15,000 Soviet Republic painters and sculptors. These were executed over the past two years.

IN AN EAST AFRICAN NEWSPAPER: A new swimming pool is rapidly taking shape since the contractors have thrown in the bulk of their workers.

IN A VIENNA HOTEL: In case of fire, do your utmost to alarm the hotel porter.

A SIGN POSTED IN GERMANY'S BLACK FOREST: It is strictly forbidden on our black forest camping site that people of different sex, for instance, men and women, live together in one tent unless they are married with each other for that purpose.

IN A ZURICH HOTEL: Because of the impropriety of entertaining guests of the opposite sex in the bedroom, it is suggested that the lobby be used for this purpose.

IN AN ADVERTISEMENT BY A HONG KONG DENTIST: Teeth extracted by the latest Methodists.

A TRANSLATED SENTENCE FROM A RUSSIAN CHESS BOOK: A lot of water has been passed under the bridge since this variation has been played.

IN A ROME LAUNDRY: Ladies, leave your clothes here and spend the afternoon having a good time.

IN A CZECHOSLOVAKIAN TOURIST AGENCY: Take one of our horse-driven city tours— we guarantee no miscarriages.

ADVERTISEMENT FOR DONKEY RIDES IN THAILAND: Would you like to ride on your own ass?

ON THE FAUCET IN A FINNISH WASHROOM: To stop the drip, turn cock to right.

IN THE WINDOW OF A SWEDISH FURRIER: Fur coats made for ladies from their own skin.

ON THE BOX OF A CLOCKWORK TOY MADE IN HONG KONG: Guaranteed to work throughout its useful life.

DETOUR SIGN IN KYUSHI, JAPAN: Stop: Drive Sideways.

IN A SWISS MOUNTAIN INN: Special today— no ice cream.

IN A BANGKOK TEMPLE: It is forbidden to enter a woman even a foreigner if dressed as a man.

IN A TOKYO BAR: Special cocktails for the ladies with nuts.

IN A COPENHAGEN AIRLINE TICKET OFFICE: We take your bags and send them in all directions.

ON THE DOOR OF A MOSCOW HOTEL ROOM: If this is your first visit to the USSR, you are welcome to it.

IN A NORWEGIAN COCKTAIL LOUNGE: Ladies are requested not to have children in the bar.

AT A BUDAPEST ZOO: Please do not feed the animals. If you have any suitable food, give it to the guard on duty.

IN THE OFFICE OF A ROMAN DOCTOR: Specialist in women and other diseases.

IN AN ACAPULCO HOTEL: The manager has personally passed all the water served here.

IN A TOKYO SHOP: Our nylons cost more than common, but you'll find they are best in the long run.

FROM A JAPANESE INFORMATION BOOKLET ABOUT USING A HOTEL AIR CONDITIONER: Cooles and Heates: If you want just condition of warm in your room, please control yourself.

FROM A BROCHURE OF A CAR RENTAL FIRM IN TOKYO: When passenger of foot heave in sight, tootle the horn. Trumpet him melodiously at first, but if he still obstacles your passage then tootle him with vigor.

TWO SIGNS FROM A MAJORCAN SHOP ENTRANCE:
— English well talking.
— Here speeching American.

**):-( Unsmiley big face**

## MIND YOUR MANNERS

Devin.E.Ben-Hur@cup.portal.com                                    true, chuckle

(An amusing anecdote from the San Jose Mercury News.)

Nearly everyone knows that Judith Martin, better known as Miss Manners, the syndicated columnist, is exceedingly correct. Last week, she saw an advertisement in the newspaper that a Maryland jewelry store was having a sale in her silver pattern. Upon arriving at the store, she told the jeweler she was looking for additional dessert spoons in her pattern and had been making do with the larger soup spoons.

"That's not much of a hardship," the employee said. *"It is for me,"* Martin responded. Caught up in the moment, the saleswoman joked, *"Who do you think you are, Miss Manners?"* The easily recognizable Miss Manners looked at the woman, unable to respond. And then it registered. *"Oh my God!"* the saleswoman said.

`)8-) Scuba Smiley big-face`

## LABORATORY EXPERIMENT

noworol@eecg.toronto.edu (Mark Noworolski)
EECG, University of Toronto                                sexual, true, funny

A friend of mine studying medicine once told me this story.

Apparently one day there was a lab where all the students were learning how to identify various cells. As samples they were using tissue scraped from the inside of the mouth.

One girl was having terrible difficulties figuring out what kind of cell she was seeing under her microscope—eventually she called over the teaching assistant to identify it.

He came over, smirked, and exclaimed, loud enough for everyone to hear, *"Oh wow! That's a sperm cell!"*

She was somewhat more careful after that experience....

## INTELLIGENCE AT GA TECH

daves@pravda.gatech.edu (Dave Smith)
Georgia Institute of Technology

true, funny

Dr. Richard LeBlanc, associate professor of ICS, was quoted in "The Technique," Georgia Tech's newspaper, last November (after the computer worm hit the net):

*"It turned out that the worm exploited three or four different holes in the system. From this, and the fact that we were able to capture and examine some of the source code, we realized that we were dealing with someone very sharp, probably not someone here on campus."*

## WINNING NUMBERS

woof@hpfcsdw.UUCP (Steve Wolfe)
Fort Collins Systems Division, Hewlett-Packard, CO

true, funny

From the Blue Springs, Missouri, Examiner:

PICK 3

ST. LOUIS— The winning numbers drawn Tuesday night in the daily Missouri Lottery Pick 3 game were 9-9-9.

A winning $1 ticket with the numbers in the correct order paid $500; a winning $1 ticket with the numbers in any order paid $160.

## WATCH WHERE YOU'RE GOING

grant@looking.on.ca (Grant Robinson)

true, chuckle

A reportedly true story heard on Q107 yesterday:

A man was driving from his home up to Thunder Bay, Ontario to visit friends. While there, he was involved in a collision with another car, but the other driver left the scene of the accident. He reported it to the police, who looked into it, and told him the next day that the car that hit him was a stolen vehicle. The man was able to drive his pickup truck home, only to find when he got home that, lo and behold, his car was stolen! Sure enough, the car that hit him several hundred miles from home was his own.

I'd just like to see if his insurance agent breaks down laughing or crying.

## LARGE RODENTS

spl@ncsc.ncsc.org (Steve Lamont)                    true, smirk

I found this blurb in the USAir Gift Catalog ("This catalog is yours to keep. Please take it with you!") recently. Quoted without permission:

GOPHER-IT

Prevent damage to garden and lawns from burrowing rodents with Gopher-It, the electronic stake that emits vibration and sound that's intensely annoying to underground rodents up to 100 feet in diameter.

Requires 4 "D" batteries, not included.

#26284 Gopher-It $49.95 (3.95)

*For rodents of greater than 100 feet in diameter you need the nuclear powered version.*

## HI! DO YOU KNOW ME? I'M THE KING OF SWEDEN.

brendan@cs.widener.edu (Brendan Kehoe)
Widener University in Chester, PA                    chuckle

[Told by sven@cs.widener.edu (Sven Heinicke) after I mentioned I finally found out that George Bush not only carries ID with him, but he also has an American Express Card.]

The King of Sweden, about one year ago, went into a computer store wanting to buy his son a computer for Christmas. He was going to pay for it with a credit card (I don't know what kind of credit card it was), and the salesman asked him for some ID. His face being on almost every 1 Kr. (1 crown) coin in Sweden (his father is on some of the old ones), he took a coin out of his pocket and put it on the table saying that that was his ID. It seems that that was not good enough and he finally took out his real ID (I guess he was being smart). But then when he was walking out of the store with the computer the anti-shoplifter alarm went off.

## SOMETHING TO THINK ABOUT

"Henry_Cate_III.PA"@XEROX.COM
Xerox, Sunnyvale, CA                    true, smirk

In a survey taken several years ago, all incoming freshman at MIT were asked if they expected to graduate in the top half of their class. Ninety-seven percent responded that they did.

## HOLIDAY PICS

carol@uunet.uu.net (Carol Gibson)

true, smirk

This is a true story...

My father and stepmother knew that my baby brother was going to have to be born by Caesarian. Nonetheless, flush with parental enthusiasm, they decided that Dad was to take photos of the event. The roll of film was duly taken and sent off to be processed, however when we got the little package back we found it to be full of someone's holiday snaps. There had been a mix-up and someone else was, at that very moment, finding photos of an operation instead of beaches and smiling faces...

When the developers arranged a swap they told us the other people had been "very upset."

## SAN FRANCISCO EARTHQUAKE (gruesome...)

bowdidge@cs.ucsd.edu (Robert Bowdidge)
CSE Dept., U.C. San Diego

true?, smirk

This sounds like an urban myth, but I trust the teller.

A friend from Berkeley just started working for the University. His supervisor had the following tale to tell:

The supervisor and his brother were going off to the 3rd game of the World Series on Oct. 17. The brother was taking his new car, a pure white Mercedes with gold trim. He'd bought it three days before.

They get to the game, park, and go to the stands. The earthquake hits. Everyone cheers. Everyone goes out to their cars. However, our two heroes can't find their car— it's been stolen. Somehow they get home, tell the insurance company, and go on with their lives.

A couple weeks ago, the insurance company phoned back saying that they'd found the car. In fact, they'd found the thief as well— he was in the car when they found it... in the Cypress Structure, crushed to six inches high...

The brother was horrified, but Andy's supervisor was really happy. "Yes, there is justice in this world!"

## PIA ZADORA
jdnicoll@watyew.waterloo.edu (James Nicoll)

true, funny

I am told that in the production of "The Diary of Anne Frank" with Pia Zadora in the title role [no, really], when the Germans showed up, looking for hidden Jews, the audience started shouting *"She's upstairs! She's upstairs!"*

Truly, an unforgettable actress.

**=:-) Smiley punk-rocker**

## PIT BULLS
jfine@cadence.com (Joel Fine)

true, funny

Seen on a bloodied, ripped T-shirt:
I LOVE MY PIT BULL.

**=:-( Real punk-rockers don't smile**

## RE: KIDS - THE NATURAL COMEDIANS
wayne@.UUCP (Wayne Hathaway)
Ultra Network Technologies

true, funny

In response to the request for "kids growing up" stories, here's one told to me many years ago by some friends about their five-year-old daughter Laura. The mother calls it "The Kevin Incident." The father just says, "Like Mother, Like Daughter."

It seems that Laura came home from Nursery School one day and announced that Kevin had pee-peed in the yard. Since Laura was one of the older children in the Nursery School group, her parents wanted to impress on her that she should try to help the younger children learn right from wrong, so they said, *"Well, Laura honey, how big is Kevin?"*

Whereupon Laura held her two index fingers an inch or so apart and said, *"Oh, about this big."*

## A FLARE FOR THE UNUSUAL

snider@inf.ethz.ch                                              true, funny

Reading jerry298's story about the life-raft in the VW inspired me to write down an incident that happened to me about 10 years ago. Like Jerry, it took me about 5 years to see the humor in it.

About 10 years ago, I bought a used van to drive back and forth to my cottage on weekends. It had previously been owned by a company called "Canada Dredge and Dock." This gave it some notoriety since they were at the time involved in a big local political scandal involving rigged bidding on dredging contracts.

One weekend at the cottage I was giving it a good cleaning out when I discovered a red cylinder labeled "Emergency Flare" in one of the door pockets. I thought "Well, that's not a bad thing to have in the car." and left it there. Sure enough, on the way home that weekend, we had a flat tire. I should say that our cottage is in the middle of a very popular vacation area north of Toronto, and the weekend in question was the combined Canadian July 1st and American July 4th holiday weekend. So the entire world was headed home on the same road.

I got out to change the tire and my brother-in-law said, *"Have you got an emergency flare in the van?"* I told him about the one I had found and he ran down the road a few hundred feet to set it up. I was under the van setting up the jack when I heard a loud pop. I looked out to see Ron running towards me yelling, *"It's a marine flare."*

That's right, Canada Dredge and Dock, being a largely marine based company, had left a marine emergency flare in their truck. In case anybody doesn't know, a marine flare is like a very powerful roman candle, shooting balls of light hundreds of feet up in the air so that drowning sailors will be seen by passing ships. They are NOT intended to be set off late at night on a busy highway.

The first ball had missed Ron's face by about 2 inches and the force had tipped the flare over onto the little mound that he had made to hold it in place. Now, as each ball came shooting out, the force would spin the flare on the little mound, so that no two went in the same direction. One of them shot right at us and passed between us as we stood no more than 5 feet apart. One of them shot back up the road at 3 lanes of oncoming traffic. One of them shot up into a farmer's field and started a small fire. Neither of us was about to go back and try to pick it up. Finally after about 7 or 8 shots, it stopped.

Amazingly, the shots that went up the highway came between platoons of traffic so nobody was hit, nobody even went off the road. Ron went and put out the fire, I changed the tire, and we drove to the nearest pull-off and sat there shaking for half an hour.

## HIGH SCHOOL NAME

seth@miro.berkeley.edu (Seth Teller)         true, smirk, sexual

PENDLETON, Ind. (AP)— Officials are considering changing the name of Pendleton Middle School or at least removing its initials from athletic uniforms to avoid embarrassment for its girls' teams.

## BAMBI'S GOT A GUN

tarsa@abyss.pa.dec.com         true, chuckle

Told to me by a friend:

We went to a party last Saturday night. One of the party-goers is friend of ours who happens to be a policeman in Wayland.

He told this story about he and a friend who went to Maine to go deer hunting. Seems they didn't get what they were after, but that was OK because they had the last laugh.

They had brought with them an inflatable, man sized doll which they dressed in hunter's clothing and tied it to the hood of their car just before leaving to return home. They also had pullover head masks that looked exactly like a deer which of course they each put on, and then drove nonchalantly down the Maine turnpike.

To say that they caused a commotion would be an understatement. They even got pulled over by a Maine State Trooper who said that they were really doing nothing wrong, but told them they were leaving a trail of accidents behind and asked them to kindly remove the costumes!

**+:-) Smiley priest**

## CHANGES IN PERCEPTIONS

njs@scifi.UUCP (Nicholas J. Simicich)                    true, computer, chuckle

Back in the early 80s, I was the only systems programmer
supporting a VM system, and I carried a beeper. I looked
disreputable, as usual, and was attending a movie (Poltergeist)
when, just before the climax, my beeper went off. I held it to
my ear, and couldn't understand the message, so I went out to
call the message center (and never saw the end of the movie).

The thing that stuck in my mind, though, was the woman two rows
behind me who turned to her friend and said, in a loud, obnoxious voice,
*"Him, he's a doctor?"*

It is almost ten years later, and I again carry a beeper, and I still go to
movies. I dread being beeped out of a movie, though. I can imagine the
loud obnoxious voice from two rows back saying, *"Him, he's a drug
dealer?"*

> **:-q Smiley trying to touch its tongue to its nose**

## FW: SECURITY NEWS UPDATE

a-marifh@microsoft.com                    true, chuckle, computer

Security news update: maybe they were here to clean the pool? (fwd)
From ... several forwards ...

Earlier this week, a Microsoft security guard caught two non-Microsoft
employees playing volleyball on our campus volleyball court and asked
them to leave the premises.

When asked by a fellow employee how he knew that the two were not
Microsoft employees, the guard replied:

*"They had tans."*

> **:-e Disappointed Smiley**

## FINDING A COP

barring@fiji.cs.umass.edu                                                   true, chuckle

My friend claims (yes, I know about urban myths) that when he was working late at the office of his family's business, he heard what sounded like a break-in in the warehouse. He called 911 (general emergency number) and got no answer. Immediately he called the local Dunkin' Donuts shop, asked to speak to a police officer, and got one over right away.

## WEDDING GIFTS, ALLEGEDLY TRUE

RICH@suhep.phy.syr.edu (Richard S. Holmes)                                   true, funny

A friend of mine claims this happened to a friend of hers:

She had a wedding to go to, and needed a wedding gift. Aha, thought she, I have that monogrammed silver tray from my wedding that I never use. I'll just take it to a silversmith and have him remove my monogram and put hers on it. Voila, one cheap wedding present.

So she took it to the silversmith and asked him to remove her monogram and put the new one on. The silversmith took a look at the tray, shook his head, and said,

*"Lady, you can only do this so many times!"*

## A POINTED WARNING

dleigh@hplabsz.hpl.hp.com (Darren Leigh)                                     true, chuckle

I found this warning on a small utility knife in MIT's lab supply:
Caution. Blade is sharp. Keep out of children.

## WHY I LOVE RADIO

PADGETT@intellicorp.com (Penny Padgett)                                      true, chuckle

Heard on radio station KKUP, Cupertino, CA:

Host: *Well, do you have any concluding statements, Marshall?*

Guest: *No, I don't, Larry.*

Host: *Then could you say something to last about three minutes?*

## A COP WITH A SENSE OF HUMOUR

mark@umbra.cc.gatech.edu (Mark J. Reed)                                   true, funny

The person I heard this from ("Al" in the story) swears that it really happened. (And no, I'm not this "Mark" - you should be able to figure out why I chose those names:)

Two guys (we'll call them "Mark" and "Al") are out cruising. Mark is driving, and they're on some out-of-the way roads. Mark is distracted and doesn't see a stop-sign, and a few moments after he runs it they hear a siren and see blue lights. Mark has never been stopped by the police before, and gets really nervous.

MARK: *OhshitwhatdidIdo? I wasn't speeding, was I? No, I wasn't speeding. What'd I do what'd I do?*

He pulls over, shaking like a leaf. The cop pulls in behind and walks up to his window.

COP: *You realize you ran a stop sign back there?*

MARK: [panicky] *No, honest! I didn't see it! I didn't mean to run it! I just didn't see it! Really!*

COP: *I'll need to see your driver's license.*

Mark pats his pants for a few seconds before remembering that he's wearing shorts with no pockets. He looks around the car, finds his wallet, opens it up, and starts frantically throwing things out of it into the back seat. No license. He enlists Al's help, and together they search the glove compartment, under the seats, behind the cushions, front and back, to no avail. After ten or fifteen minutes of searching, Al looks up and catches the officer's eye.

AL: *You don't need to see his identification.*

COP: [without missing a beat] *I don't need to see his identification.*

AL: *These aren't the droids you're looking for.*

COP: *These aren't the droids we're looking for.*

AL: *He may go on about his business.*

COP: *You may go on about your business.*

AL: *Move along.*

COP: *Move along.*

At this point the cop turns around, walks back to his car, gets in, and drives away.

Mark pulls out and makes it about 200 yards down the road. Then he stops and just shakes for a few minutes, finally asking Al to drive.

## REALITY! WHAT A CONCEPT!

bill@twwells.com (T. William Wells)                              chuckle, true

According to a film my wife saw in her philosophy class, Bertrand Russell received a letter from a woman who proclaimed herself a solipsist. She went on to say that she was surprised that there weren't more solipsists.

`:-t cross smiley`

## DIPLOMACY WITH THE POLICE II

dnwiebe@cis.ohio-state.edu (Dan N Wiebe)                         true, funny

My brother's psychology professor, a Yankee's Yankee and a feminist's feminist, tells the following story on herself to illustrate that doctorates don't necessarily make you smart.

She was driving to a workshop in Atlanta from her home in Ohio. It was about 10 am, and she'd been driving the entire preceding day and night herself, and she was consequently not in the best of tempers as she searched for a motel in which to crash.

A Georgia state policeman pulled her over, got out of his cruiser, swaggered up to her driver's window, bent down, and drawled, *"Lookie here, darlin',"*—uh oh, everybody duck—*"Lookie here, darlin', nobody blows through Georgia that fast."*

Said the feminist Yankee overtired psychology professor: *"Sherman did."*

She says he was not satisfied merely to give her a speeding ticket; he made her follow him fifty miles out of her way to Nowheresburg, GA, and wait at the police station until three in the afternoon for a circuit judge to arrive so that he could explain to her why it wasn't the best idea in the world to be impolite to policemen, who were after all interested only in creating the safest possible environment for everybody including her, etc. etc. The lecture went on for about two hours, she says, after which she was released to drive the fifty miles back to her route and resume her search for someplace to crash.

True story—anyway, that's what my brother said.

## ANECDOTES ON OLD INSTITUTIONS
msb@sq.com (Mark Brader)

true, smirk

-From: credmond@watmath.waterloo.edu (Chris Redmond)
Marc Riese writes:

I agree that The Bay is a very special company for Canada for its long and "colourful" history, but I think it's a youngster in comparison to certain European companies (although I couldn't name one). I remember hearing a story of an American company negotiating a business deal with a Swedish steel company. In the proposition sent to Europe, the American company mentioned some reliability concerns and asked for proof that they could count on the Swedish company still being there in a year. In a terse letter, the Swedish firm replied that since they had existed more than four times the age of the USA, they didn't see why they would not be there the next year...

Comparable anecdote #1: At the 350th anniversary celebrations of Harvard University, one speaker said, *"Harvard is intimately bound up with the history and culture of the United States— an innovation in which we have taken considerable interest."*

Comparable anecdote #2: Someone has calculated that there are in Europe 26 (this number is my best recollection of what was said) organizations that have been in continuous existence for at least five hundred years: the Parliament at Westminster, the Althing (parliament) of Iceland, the Roman Catholic Church, and 23 universities.

-From: brad@looking.on.ca (Your Editor)

Anecdote #3, told by Greg Benford: At an Oxford college, they were debating what to do with all their money. The consensus was to buy land, since *"for the past thousand years, land has proven to be a very wise investment for the college."*

The crusty old patriarch piped in, *"True, but the past thousand years have been atypical."*

**:-i Semi-smiley**

## MORE ANECDOTES ON OLD INSTITUTIONS.

dgil@ipsaint.ipsa.reuter.com (Gillett, David)
Reuters Information Services (Canada)                                    true, chuckle

My two favourite anecdotes on this subject demonstrate the difference between renewable and non-renewable resources. First the non-renewable:

The congregation of a small stone church (in England?) decided that the stone which formed the step up to the front door had become too worn by its years of use, and would have to be replaced. Unfortunately, there were hardly any funds available for the replacement. Then someone came up with the bright idea that the replacement could be postponed for many years by simply turning the block of stone over.

They discovered that their great-grandparents had beaten them to it.

Now the renewable:

An entomologist at New College, Oxford ("New" because it's only a few centuries old), discovered beetles infesting the oak beams supporting the roof of the Great Hall. It was fairly urgent that these be replaced before the roof collapsed— but anyone who has looked at the price of oak lately can tell you that this was not something the college budget was prepared for.

Since oak from a commercial supplier was out of the question, someone suggested that the college Forester be sent for. His job was to administer the various scattered tracts of land that had been deeded to the college when it was founded. The trustees hoped he might know of suitable trees on college land.

It turned out that there was indeed a suitable stand of mighty oaks. They had been planted when the college was founded, and down the centuries each Forester had told his successor: *"You don't cut those oaks; those are for when the beetles get into the beams in the Main Hall."*

:-[ Unsmiley blockhead

## RADIO SHACK Q&A

jdwren@aardvark.ucs.uoknor.edu (Jonathan)
University of Oklahoma - University Computing Services                  original, laugh, true

Do these guys at Radio Shack ever get on your nerves, asking you for a bunch of personal data when you're just there to buy something as simple as a couple AA batteries? I think we should inconvenience these people as much as they do us. A while ago I was in Enid buying a printer cable adaptor and the guy asked me for my name.

*"Ghosseindhatsghabyfaird-johnson,"* I replied.

(blank look of confusion)

*"How do you spell that?"* he asked, obviously not wanting to know.

*"With a hyphen,"* I clarified

*"Once more?"* he asked

*"Ghosseindhatsghabyfaird-johnson"*

*"Could you please spell that?"* he asked, glancing at the half dozen people waiting behind me.

*"Oh... just like it sounds,"* I said nonchalantly.

Putting down "Johnson," he went on and asked about the address.

*"Washburn, Wisconsin, 14701 N.E. Wachatanoobee Parkway, Complex 3, Building O, Appt. 1382b,"* I replied.

Almost through writing all this down, I said, *"Or did you mean current address?"*

Stopping, he said, (becoming irritated) *"Yes. Current address."*

*"Diluthian Heights, Mississippi, 1372 S. Tinatonabee Avenue, Building 14C, Suite 2, Box 138201,"* I replied quite slowly.

Waiting until he finished I said, *"No, wait, it's NORTH Tinatonabee Avenue."* Annoyed, he backed up and changed it.

*"I think,"* I interjected.

*"And is all this correct?"* he asked in a standard manner.

*"Of course not,"* I replied, leaving, *"If you want my REAL name and address, look at the damned credit card receipt."*

A little mean, I must admit, but no jury would convict me... at least, none that had been to Radio Shack.

**:-p Smiley sticking its tongue out (at you!)**